Michael M. Dediu

All Wars and Conflicts are due to HUMAN ERRORS

Moving from perpetual war errors, to friendly collaboration and peace

---

DERC Publishing House
Nashua, New Hampshire, U. S. A.

Published and printed in the
United States of America
On the Great Seal of the United States are included:
E Pluribus Unum (Out of many, one)
Annuit Coeptis (He has approved of the undertakings)
Novus Ordo Seclorum (New order of the ages)

Library of Congress Control Number: 2021911380

Dediu, Michael M.

All Wars and Conflicts are due to HUMAN ERRORS
Moving from perpetual war errors, to friendly collaboration and peace

ISBN-13: 978-1-950999-39-2

MSG0664400_8776h9fYKmjYE4K2XmFk
1-10560650591
1-4UNJE76
1-4UNJE7X
00503D
26SDANAO

Preface

There are tens of thousands of wars and conflicts in history – practically there are perpetual wars and conflicts all the time – and all of them are due to enormous human errors! All people want to immediately stop these non-sense errors, and start a normal life, based on peace, no arms, freedom, good health, good education, good jobs, harmony and prosperity for all on our beloved Earth!

Why these perennial war errors persisted for so long? There are many fundamental questions that all human beings are called to answer. The most important philosophers, including Socrates, Plato, Aristotle, Descartes, and Kant, always asked profound questions, and gave eternal answers.

Over 140 years ago, around 1881, Darwin said "To kill an error is as good a service as, and sometimes even better than, the establishing of a new truth or fact." Yes, we need to eliminate these never-ending war errors – it is well known, for over 2000 years, the Latin maxim "errare humanum est, perseverare diabolicum" (to err is human, to persist is diabolical" – and this diabolical simply means due to illness.

This book presents many war errors from history, using questions, clearly showing how bad the war errors are, and comparing with new ideas, which will create the conditions for a peaceful, free, healthy, harmonious and prosperous life for all on our Peaceful Terra.

The future begins to take shape in front of our eyes, and is amazingly attractive!

Michael M. Dediu, Ph. D.

Nashua, New Hampshire, U. S. A., 12 June 2021

USA, the University of California, Berkeley (1868, named after the philosopher and mathematician Bishop George Berkeley (1685-1753), motto Fiat lux (Let there be light), 36,200 students, major public research university, 72 Nobel laureates, between the top six universities in the world, 500 ha campus), il Campanile (Sather Tower (61 bells (full concert carillon) and clock tower). 1914, 94 m, 7 floors, observation deck on the 8th floor, inspired by il Campanile (850, 1514, 1912, 99 m) di San Marco (1084), Venezia (421, Venice), Italy (900 BC)).

Table of Contents

Question 1. What is needed to correct these dangerous human errors, started over 4,800 years ago?

Response 1. Over 4,800 years ago, around 2800 BC, about 80 km south of Baghdad, the leaders of Kish and Elam had a war, because of their mistakes.

They should have started to think about living in peace and harmony – we did, and created the new Constitution of the World, whose objective is simply to help all the people on Earth to live better, peacefully, free, healthy, harmoniously, and prosperously.

More precisely, the Constitution starts with 7 details about its objectives:

We, the People on this Earth, in order to

1.1 - completely eliminate war and any type of conflicts,

1.2 - have a peaceful and harmonious world,

1.3 - have freedom, dignity, good families and respect,

1.4 - have good health and good education,

1.5 - have a friendly atmosphere and prosperity,

1.6 – have the safety and wellbeing of all the people in the world as the highest priority,

1.7 – use the best peaceful results, experience and knowledge of all current countries,

establish this Constitution of the World.

Italy, Venezia: Piazza San Marco with Palazzo Ducale (right), Libreria Sansoviniana (next to Palazzo Ducale), Basilica di San Marco (back), Giardini Reali and Il Campanile (center-right), Procuratie Nuove (center to left), Capitano di Porto (left).

USA, New York (1624): on Broadway, looking at 7th Ave. in Times Square, close to Times Square Tower (2004, 221 m, 47 floors).

Question 2. Is peace a priority around 2600 BC?

Response 2. No - around 2600 BC there were the war campaigns errors of Sneferu from Egypt against Nubia, Libya and Levant.

Now peace is the first priority – without peace not much can be done.

From the Shard (244 m), looking west to (from right down): railroad bridge (Cannon St Station), Southwalk Bridge, Millennium Bridge, another railroad bridge, Blackfriars Bridge, and Waterloo Bridge.

Italy, Venezia, in the middle of the west façade of the Basilica di San Marco, we see the central bronze-fashioned door, in a round-arched portal, encircled by polychrome marble columns. Above this door there are three round bas-relief cycles of Romanesque art. A Japanese couple, with their Japanese photographer, make their wedding photographs in this most beautiful place.

Question 3. On what people should have started to work around 2500 BC, instead of making grave errors?

Response 3. Around 2500 BC there were the war campaigns errors of Eannatum from Lagash (a city state in the present Iraq) against Umma and other neighbors. Then Umma started wars against Lagash in 2450 BC, 2400 BC, and 2350 BC

It would have been nice to start thinking that all the people of the world will be proud citizens of only one country, called Peaceful Terra, with total area of over 509 M km^2, and land area over 148 M km^2.

Being just one country, there are no borders:

USA, New York (1624): on 7th Avenue in Times Square, close to the W 43rd Street, and to Times Square Tower (2004, 221 m, 47 floors).

Question 4. Were they thinking about the number of rules around 2279 BC, to avoid errors?

Response 4. No, around 2279 BC the Akkadian Empire (Mesopotamia) was formed by wars against the neighbors.

Regarding the rules - not too many is much better:
All the rules – not more than 2,000, on maximum 1,000 pages - on our Earth will be established by the people and their elected Advisers.

All rules proposed by Advisers must be approved by their 5 assistants (doctors, mathematicians, CEOs, engineers and teachers), and for any new rule over 2,000 basic rules (each rule on at most half a page, total 1,000 pages), at least on old rule must be eliminated.

All the rules can be changed or eliminated when a majority of the people or their Advisors agree, but some fundamental peace and order rules will remain.

Question 5. Was the administration of Terra in the minds of people around 2112 BC?

Response 5. Well, no – they just had another example of errors: around 2112 BC Ur-Nammu occupied Lagash by war, creating the Neo-Sumerian Empire, which fell 108 years letter, in 2004 BC.

Peaceful Terra, being a very big country, will be divided in 10 simple regions:

For easier administration, Peaceful Terra will be only administratively divided in 10 simple and friendly regions of around 770 M people each, called R0, R1,…, R9, which will be delimited by meridians (or line of longitudes), with the assistance of the United Nations.

USA, UC Berkeley (1868), from Campanile (1914, 94 m) looking northwest: Mathematics Dep. (right middle), Transportation Inst. (center right), and Bancroft Library (down center).

Question 6. Was somebody in Babylon thinking where will the capital of this Peaceful Terra be?

Response 6. Unfortunately, no, they were busy making errors - around 1763 BC Hammurabi from Babylon occupied by war Larsa, Assyria, and other neighbors – the Babylonian Empire fell 168 years later, in 1595 BC.

The capital can be everywhere! Because the capitals tend to become huge bureaucracies, with lots of people trying to be there, without much usefulness, Peaceful Terra will have moving capitals, to benefit everybody.

Each region will have a pair of capitals plus an outside city, for better and more homogenous management (all will change every year; more details are in the annex book "World with One Country & its Ten Friendly Regions - Moving from 195 disagreeing countries, to 1 country with 10 collaborating regions"). For example, the first implementation will be:
R0 between meridians 0 and 15^0 E, capitals: Bern (Switzerland), Libreville (Gabon), and Oxford (UK).
R1: 15^0 E - 30^0 E, Warsaw (Poland), Pretoria (South Africa) and Miami (FL, USA).
R2: 30^0 E - 45^0 E, Moscow (Russia), Cairo (Egypt), and Grenoble (France).
R3: 45^0 E - 75^0 E, Astana (Kazakhstan), Karachi (Pakistan), and Montpellier (France).
R4: 75^0 E - 85^0 E, New Delhi (India), Novosibirsk (Russia), and Magdeburg (Germany).
R5: 85^0 E - 100^0 E, Krasnoyarsk (Russia), Urumqi (China), and Avignon (France).
R6: 100^0 E - 115^0 E, Jakarta (Indonesia), Beijing (China), and Neuchâtel (Switzerland).
R7: 115^0 E - 180^0, Tokyo (Japan), Sydney (Australia), and Malmö (Sweden).

R8: 180^0 - 70^0 Washington (USA), Mexico City (Mexico), and Bellinzona (Switzerland).
R9: 70^0 W – 0 Halifax (Canada), Brasilia (Brazil), and Biel (Switzerland).

France, Paris: Monument to Alfred de Musset (1810 – 1857, dramatist) in Parc Monceau, (1779, 8.2 ha), on Boulevard de Courcelles.

In the first implementation, there are many big differences between the populations of different regions, and then between the populations of different sub-regions, but this is just the first implementation, which needs to be quickly put in place, and then, very easily, the delimitations will be moved a few kilometers east or west, to reach a balanced population.

Because all the people are in the same country, it is normal to modify a little its regions, for better administration, to make everybody happy.

It is well understood that there will be some difficulties in the beginning, like in all beginnings, but with calm, patience, perseverance and hard work, the things will improve fast, and all the people will enjoy a better life.

USA, New York (1624): on 7th Avenue in Times Square, close to the W 43rd Street, and to Times Square Tower (2004, 221 m, 47 floors).

Question 7. Around 1675 BC, was there any thinking about how many subdivisions will be in each Region?

Response 7. Regrettably not, just errors - around 1675 BC Shang rebel forces had a war against the Xia Dynasty in China.

Each of the 10 regions will be divided by meridians in 10 sub-regions S00, , S99, each with about 77 M people.

Then each of the 100 sub-regions will be divided in 10 districts:

Each of the 100 sub-regions will be divided in 10 districts D000, D001, , D999, each with about 7.7 M people, and each of the districts will have their current small and big cities.

All these delimitations between regions, as well as between sub-regions, will be flexible:

There will be just simple administrative delimitations, and all these delimitations between regions, as well as between sub-regions, will be flexible – they will be changed after each census (5 years), for maintaining a balanced number of people in all regions (around 770 M) and sub-regions (around 77 M).

Question 8. Around 1506 BC, any thinking about the meridians used for divisions?

Response 8: Sadly no - for 78 years, between 1506 BC and 1428 BC there were long wars of Thutmose I, Thutmose II, and Thutmose III from the Egyptian Empire against Nubia, the neighbor to the south.

Meridians are easy to use, impartial, helpful for people with telework:

Having telework, many people will have a northern residence and a southern residence, seasonally moving from one to the other, to avoid extreme cold or heat, and having the same hour.

Finland, Helsinki: in the south of the Railway Square is the Ateneum (1887, a major museum of classical art).

Question 9. In 1457 BC, how was the harmony between Egypt and Syria?

Response 9: Because of numerous errors, no harmony yet - for 21 years, between 1457 BC and 1436 BC, Thutmose III from the Egyptian Empire had 17 wars against Syria.

Harmony is essential - all the oceans will belong to some of the regions, and working harmoniously to maintain and clean the oceans will give beautiful results:

All the oceans will belong to some of the regions defined above, therefore will be maintained by those regions, to be free of any piracy or other bad activity – World Police will help when necessary.

The harmony will generate strong cooperation for the maintenance of the oceans, which will also become residence for many people.

Question 10. In 1278 BC, any initiatives about the World Government?

Response 10: Not yet, just errors - for 18 years, between 1278 BC and 1260 BC, Ramesses II of Egypt had over 4 wars with Syria, and several wars with Hittite Empire (now Turkey), Nubia, and other neighbors.

The family of over 7. 7 B people from Peaceful Terra will have four levels of world management; at the local level, if needed, it could be one or two more levels of local managers (mayors, town managers, county managers – all levels of management must be friendly, helpful, fast, polite, modest and smart):

Level 1 Management: 1,000 L1 friendly managers, for the 1,000 districts, who will supervise and assist the mayors and town managers from their district, for a total of about 7,700,000 people in each district. Each of the 1,000 L1 friendly managers will be located in a central city from their districts – they could be the mayors of those cities, but with new responsibilities for the whole district.

Level 2 Management: 100 L2 friendly managers, for the 100 sub-regions, who will supervise and assist the 10 L1 managers of the 10 districts of each sub-region, for a total of about 77,000,000 people for each sub-region. These 100 L2 friendly managers will move each month between the two capitals of each of the 100 sub-regions.

Italy, Venezia, Libreria Sansoviniana (left), La Loggetta (center-left down), Il Campanile (center), and Procuratie Nuove (right). Il Campanile della Basilica di San Marco (1156 – 1173, last restored in 1514), rebuilt in 1912 *com'era, dov'era* (as it was, where it was) after the collapse of the original campanile on 14 July 1902. Adjacent to the Campanile, facing towards the Basilica, is the small building known as La Loggetta, built by Sansovino in 1537 – 1546.

Question 11. In 1260 BC, are Troy, Sparta and Athens thinking about now to choose the two capitals for each sub-region?

Response 11: No, because of errors - for 80 years, between 1260 BC and 1180 BC, there was the well-known (because of Homer's Iliad and Odyssey (around 800 BC, 400 years after the war) Trojan War, between Achaeans (Greeks from Mycenae (120 km southwest of Athens) and Sparta (southern Greece)), and Troy (or Ilium, city south of Dardanelles, now in Turkey).

Discussing with people in a harmonious atmosphere and understanding each other, will certainly help to choose, in the beginning, these capitals:

In Region R0: from Paris (France) to N'Djamena (Chad)

- The sub-region R00 will have the capitals Paris (France) and Niamey (Niger) – assistance from Magdeburg (Germany).
- The sub-region R01 will have the capitals Brussels (Belgium) and Porto-Novo (Benin) - assistance from Toronto (Canada).
- The sub-region R02 will have the capitals Amsterdam (Netherlands) and Algiers (Algeria) - assistance from Graz (Austria).
- The sub-region R03 will have the capitals Luxembourg (Luxembourg) and Sao Tome (Sao Tome and Principe) - assistance from Adelaide (Australia).
- The sub-region R04 will have the capitals of Abuja (Nigeria) and Bochum (Germany) - assistance from Nikko (Japan).
- The sub-region R05 will have the capitals Malabo (Equatorial Guinea), and Zürich (Switzerland) - assistance from Leeds (UK).
- The sub-region R06 will have the capitals Oslo (Norway) and Tunis (Tunisia) - assistance from Sheffield (UK).

- The sub-region R07 will have the capitals Roma (Italy) and Luanda (Angola) - assistance from Yamagata (Japan).
- The sub-region R08 will have the capitals in Berlin (Germany) and Tripoli (Libya) - assistance from New York (USA).
- The sub-region R09 will have the capitals Prague (Czech Republic) and N'Djamena (Chad) - assistance from Brisbane (Australia).

France, Paris: The south-west façade of Palais de Chaillot (1937, left) and the north-west side of Tour Eiffel (1889, 324 m), from Place du Trocadéro et du 11 Novembre.

In Region R1: from Zagreb (Croatia) to Bujumbura (Burundi)

- The sub-region R10 will have the capitals in Zagreb (Croatia) and Brazzaville (Congo) - assistance from Nantes (France).
- The sub-region R11 will have the capitals in Vienna (Austria), Windhoek (Namibia) - assistance from Bilbao (Spain).
- The sub-region R12 will have the capitals in Stockholm (Sweden), Bangui (Central African Republic) - assistance from Florence (Italy).
- The sub-region R13 will have the capitals in Budapest (Hungary), Rundu (Namibia) - assistance from Monaco (Monaco).
- The sub-region R14 will have the capitals in Belgrade (Serbia), Kananga (Democratic Republic of Congo) - assistance from Liverpool (UK).
- The sub-region R15 will have the capitals in Athens (Greece), Mongu (Zambia) - assistance from Los Angeles (CA, USA).
- The sub-region R16 will have the capitals in Helsinki (Finland) and Kolwezi (Democratic Republic of the Congo) - assistance from Montreal (Canada).
- The sub-region R17 will have the capitals in Bucharest (Romania) and Gaborone (Botswana) - assistance from Philadelphia (PA, USA).
- The sub-region R18 will have the capitals in Minsk (Belarus) and Maseru (Lesotho) - assistance from Orleans (France).
- The sub-region R19 will have the capitals in Chisinau (Republic of Moldova) and Bujumbura (Burundi) - assistance from Hamburg (Germany).

Japan, Tokyo Skytree - a broadcasting, restaurant, and observation tower located in Sumida, Tokyo. It became the tallest structure in Japan in 2010 and reached its full height of 634 m in March 2011, making it the tallest tower in the world, and the second tallest structure in the world. The tower opened to the public on 22 May 2012. Without antenna it is 495 m, top observation floor is at 451.2 m, and the second observation floor is at 350 m. It has 13 elevators. The exterior lattice is painted a color called "Skytree White". This is an original color based on a bluish white traditional Japanese color (aijiro). The tower is illuminated using LED lights.

In Region R2: from Kiev (Ukraine) to Baghdad (Iraq)

- The sub-region R20 will have the capitals in Kiev (Ukraine) and Kigali (Rwanda) - assistance from Ottawa (Canada).
- The sub-region R21 will have the capitals in Ankara (Turkey) and Khartoum (Sudan) - assistance from Salzburg (Austria).
- The sub-region R22 will have the capitals in Lilongwe (Malawi) and Nicosia (Cyprus) - assistance from Dallas (TX, USA).
- The sub-region R23 will have the capitals in Jerusalem (Israel) and Dodoma (Tanzania) - assistance from Strasbourg (France).
- The sub-region R24 will have the capitals in Damascus (Syria) and Nairobi (Kenya) - assistance from Stuttgart (Germany).
- The sub-region R25 will have the capitals in Krasnodar (Russia) and Addis Ababa (Ethiopia) - assistance from Marseille (France).
- The sub-region R26 will have the capitals in Rostov-on-Don (Russia) and Asmara (Eritrea) - assistance from Leipzig (Germany).
- The sub-region R27 will have the capitals in Stavropol (Russia) and Djibouti (Djibouti) - assistance from Zürich (Switzerland).
- The sub-region R28 will have the capitals in Mosul (Iraq) and Moroni (Comoros) - assistance from Linz (Austria).
- The sub-region R29 will have the capitals in Yerevan (Armenia) and Baghdad (Iraq) - assistance from Göttingen (Germany).

Italy, a modern dancing girls sculpture from Pompeii (650 BC, ancient Roman town, with a complex water system, an amphitheater, gymnasium and a port, 20 km southeast of Naples, 10 km southeast of Mount Vesuvius, mostly destroyed and buried (11,000 people) under 4 to 6 m of ash and pumice in the eruption of Mount Vesuvius in 79 AD. Now there is a vast archaeological site with excavated ruins of the ancient Pompeii, and a new modern Pompei around it).

In Region R3: from Riyadh (Saudi Arabia) to Malé (Maldives)

- The sub-region R30 will have the capitals in Riyadh (Saudi Arabia) and Mogadishu (Somalia) - assistance from Bonn (Germany).
- The sub-region R31 will have the capitals in Baku (Azerbaijan) and Antananarivo (Madagascar) - assistance from Le Mans (France).
- The sub-region R32 will have the capitals in Oral (Kazakhstan) and Tehran (Iran) - assistance from Pisa (Italy).
- The sub-region R33 will have the capitals in Ashgabat (Turkmenistan) and Abu Dhabi (United Arab Emirates) - assistance from Wolfsburg (Germany).
- The sub-region R34 will have the capitals in Magnitogorsk (Russia) and Muscat (Oman) - assistance from Toulouse (France).
- The sub-region R35 will have the capitals in Chelyabinsk (Russia) and Herat (Afghanistan) - assistance from Basel (Switzerland).
- The sub-region R36 will have the capitals in Tyumen (Russia) and Kandahar (Afghanistan) - assistance from Nagoya (Japan).
- The sub-region R37 will have the capitals in Dushanbe (Tajikistan) and Labytnangi (Russia) - assistance from Limoges (France).
- The sub-region R38 will have the capitals in Tashkent (Uzbekistan) and Kabul (Afghanistan) - assistance from Rostock (Germany).
- The sub-region R39 will have the capitals in Islamabad (Pakistan) and Malé (Maldives) - assistance from La Rochelle (France).

London, from the Shard (2012, 309 m, observatory at 244 m), looking east to the Tower Bridge (1886-1894, combined bascule and suspension turreted bridge over River Thames (flowing from west (left) to east (right)), between London boroughs Tower Hamlets (north – left up) and Southwark (south – right), length 244 m, height 65 m, longest span 82 m, clearance 8 m (closed), 42 m (open)), City Hall (2002, height 45 m, center right round, for the Greater London Authority: Mayor of London and the London Assembly).

In Region R4: from Bishkek (Kyrgyzstan) to Brahmapur (India)

- The sub-region R40 will have the capitals in Bishkek (Kyrgyzstan) and Jaipur (India) - assistance from Osaka (Japan).
- The sub-region R41 will have the capitals in Akola (India) and Kashgar (China) - assistance from Genoa (Italy).
- The sub-region R42 will have the capitals in Almaty (Kazakhstan) and Coimbatore (India) - assistance from Perth (Australia).
- The sub-region R43 will have the capitals in Kuybyshev (Russia) and Agra (India) - assistance from Fukuoka (Japan).
- The sub-region R44 will have the capitals in Vertikos (Russia) and Nagpur (India) - assistance from Coral Bay (Australia).
- The sub-region R45 will have the capitals in Chennai (India) and Colombo (Sri Lanka) - assistance from Sapporo (Japan).
- The sub-region R46 will have the capitals in Lucknow (India) and Fedosikha (Russia) - assistance from Niigata (Japan).
- The sub-region R47 will have the capitals in Bilaspur (India) and Kolpashevo (Russia) - assistance from Albany (Australia).
- The sub-region R48 will have the capitals in Visakhapatnam (India) and Barnaul (Russia) - assistance from Hiroshima (Japan).
- The sub-region R49 will have the capitals in Brahmapur (India) and Tomsk (Russia) - assistance from Yokohama (Japan).

In Region R5: from Kathmandu (Nepal) to Dehong (China)

- The sub-region R50 will have the capitals in Kathmandu (Nepal) and Patna (India) - assistance from Kobe (Japan).
- The sub-region R51 will have the capitals in Bayingol (China) and Novokuznetsk (Russia) - assistance from Vichy (France).
- The sub-region R52 will have the capitals in Thimphu (Bhutan) and Dhaka (Bangladesh) - assistance from Jena (Germany).
- The sub-region R53 will have the capitals in Lhasa (China) and Achinsk (Russia) - assistance from Reims (France).
- The sub-region R54 will have the capitals in Abakan (Russia) and Kumul (China) - assistance from Fribourg (Switzerland).
- The sub-region R55 will have the capitals in Kyzyl (Russia) and Dibrugarh (India) - assistance from Denmark (Australia).
- The sub-region R56 will have the capitals in Bassein (Myanmar) and Tinsukia (India) - assistance from Chiba (Japan).
- The sub-region R57 will have the capitals in Yushu City (China) and Tinskoy (Russia) - assistance from Klagenfurt (Austria).
- The sub-region R58 will have the capitals in Jiuquan (China) and Medan (Indonesia) - assistance from Lucerne (Switzerland).
- The sub-region R59 will have the capitals in Chiang Mai (Thailand) and Dehong (China) - assistance from Mulhouse (France).

Italy, Roma (753 BC, one of the oldest occupied cities in Europe, called Roma Aeterna (The Eternal City) and Caput Mundi (Capital of the World)), southeast of Piazza del Popolo (1822, by Giuseppe Valadier, inside the northern gate in the Aurelian Walls, the Porta Flaminia, now called the Porta del Popolo), near Via del Babuino (opened in 1525 as the Via Paolina) and the church Santa Maria in Montesanto (1679, begun by Rainaldi and completed by Bernini and Fontana), the statue of the Goddess of Abundance.

UK, London, from the Shard (2012, 309 m, observatory at 244 m), looking south to new residential and office buildings.

In Region R6: from Bangkok (Thailand) to Chita (Russia)

- The sub-region R60 will have the capitals in Bangkok (Thailand) and Kuala Lumpur (Malaysia) - assistance from Besançon (France).
- The sub-region R61 will have the capitals in Vientiane (Laos) and Singapore – assistance from Freiburg im Breisgau (Germany).
- The sub-region R62 will have the capitals in Phnom Penh (Cambodia) and Irkutsk (Russia) – assistance from Baden (Switzerland).
- The sub-region R63 will have the capitals in Palembang (Indonesia), Hanoi (Vietnam) – assistance from Thun (Switzerland).
- The sub-region R64 will have the capitals in Ulan Bator (Mongolia) and Ulan-Ude (Russia) – assistance from Chaumont (France).
- The sub-region R65 will have the capitals in Cirebon (Indonesia) and Nanning (China) – assistance from Vaduz (Lichtenstein).
- The sub-region R66 will have the capitals in Pontianak (Indonesia) and Baotou (China) – assistance from Lugano (Switzerland).
- The sub-region R67 will have the capitals in Surakarta (Indonesia) and Yichang (China) – assistance from Thonon-les-Bain (France).
- The sub-region R68 will have the capitals in Surabaya (Indonesia) and Changsha (China) – assistance from Burgdorf (Switzerland).
- The sub-region R69 will have the capitals in Chita (Russia) and Hong Kong (China) – assistance from Colmar (France).

Italy, Naples (Napoli, 1500 BC, one of the oldest continuously inhabited cities in the world. The city was refunded as Neápolis around 550 BC, and became a sine qua non of Magna Graecia), the FVNICOLARE building near downtown. The Funicolare Centrale (Central Funicular) is a funicular railway, which is the main part of the metro system for the city of Naples (1928, 1.2 km).

In Region R7: from Nanchang (China) to Melbourne (Australia)

- The sub-region R70 will have the capitals in Bandar Seri Begawan (Brunei Darussalam) and Nanchang (China) – assistance from Turku (Finland).
- The sub-region R71 will have the capitals in Krasnokamensk (Russia) and Jinan (China) – assistance from St. Gallen (Switzerland).
- The sub-region R72 will have the capitals in Baguio City (Philippines) and Hangzhou (China) – assistance from Dole (France).
- The sub-region R73 will have the capitals in Manila (Philippines) and Taipei (Taiwan, China) – assistance from Metz (France).
- The sub-region R74 will have the capitals in Kupang (Indonesia) and Shanghai (China) – assistance from Davos (Switzerland).
- The sub-region R75 will have the capitals in Pyongyang (North Korea) and Seoul (South Korea) – assistance from Versailles (France).
- The sub-region R76 will have the capitals in Vladivostok (Russia) and Busan (South Korea) – assistance from Innsbruck (Austria).
- The sub-region R77 will have the capitals in Kyoto (Japan) and Khabarovsk (Russia) – assistance from Germering (Germany).
- The sub-region R78 will have the capitals in Nagoya (Japan) and Komsomolsk-on-Amur (Russia) – assistance from Venice (Italy).
- The sub-region R79 will have the capitals in Sendai (Japan) and Melbourne (Australia) – assistance from St. Moritz (Switzerland).

Italy, Venezia, the left door on the west façade of Basilica Cattedrale Patriarcale di San Marco. Above the door we can see the Winged Lion, the symbol of St. Mark and of Venice, which holds the book quoting *"Pax Tibi Marce Evangelista Meus"* (Peace to you Mark my evangelist).

In Region R8: from Anchorage (Alaska, USA) to Lima (Peru)

- The sub-region R80 will have the capitals in Uelen (Russia) and Anchorage (Alaska, USA), – assistance from Zug (Switzerland).
- The sub-region R81 will have the capitals in Vancouver (Canada) and San Jose (CA, USA) – assistance from Odense (Denmark).
- The sub-region R82 will have the capitals in Vernon (Canada) and Los Angeles (CA, USA) – assistance from Amstetten (Austria).
- The sub-region R83 will have the capitals in Calgary (Canada) and Tijuana (Mexico) – assistance from Chur (Switzerland).
- The sub-region R84 will have the capitals in Hermosillo (Mexico) and Tucson (AR, USA) – assistance from Bergen (Norway).
- The sub-region R85 will have the capitals in Chihuahua (Mexico) and Regina (Canada) – assistance from Gothenburg (Sweden).
- The sub-region R86 will have the capitals in San Luis Potosi City (Mexico) and Winnipeg (Canada) – assistance from Yverdon-les-Bains (Switzerland).
- The sub-region R87 will have the capitals in Tulsa (OK, USA) and Veracruz (Mexico) – assistance from Bregenz (Austria).
- The sub-region R88 will have the capitals in Memphis (TN, USA) and San José (Costa Rica) – assistance from Uppsala (Sweden).
- The sub-region R89 will have the capitals in Lima (Peru) and Boston (MA, USA) – assistance from Tampere (Finland).

Italy, Rome (753 BC), Piazza di Monte Citorio, Camera dei Deputati (back), from Via della Guglia the view of the Obelisk of Montecitorio (or Solare, 21.79 m, 33.97 m with base and globe, moved here in 1789): an ancient Egyptian red granite obelisk of Psammetichus II (595-589 BC) from Heliopolis, brought to Rome with the Flaminian obelisk in 10 BC by the Roman Emperor Augustus (63 BC – 14 AD) to be used as the gnomon (the part of a sundial that casts the shadow) of the Solarium (or Horologium) Augusti (10 BC, functioned as a giant Solar clock, built by the mathematician Facondius Novus (circa 50 BC – 15 AD).

In Region R9: from La Paz (Bolivia) to London (United Kingdom)

- The sub-region R90 will have the capitals in La Paz (Bolivia) and Bangor (Maine, USA) – assistance from Aosta (Italy).
- The sub-region R91 will have the capitals in Caracas (Venezuela) and Road Town (British Virgin Islands) – assistance from Obergoms (Switzerland).
- The sub-region R92 will have the capitals in Buenos Aires (Argentina) and Fort-de-France (Martinique) – assistance from Freudenstadt (Germany).
- The sub-region R93 will have the capitals in Asuncion (Paraguay) and Montevideo (Uruguay) – assistance from Winterthur (Switzerland).
- The sub-region R94 will have the capitals in Cayenne (French Guiana), St. John's (Canada) – assistance from Novara (Italy).
- The sub-region R95 will have the capitals in Rio de Janeiro (Brazil) and Dakar (Senegal) – assistance from Toyama (Japan).
- The sub-region R96 will have the capitals in Freetown (Sierra Leone) and Lisbon (Portugal) – assistance from Kawasaki (Japan).
- The sub-region R97 will have the capitals in Bamako (Mali) and Athlone (Ireland) – assistance from Ulm (Germany).
- The sub-region R98 will have the capitals in Yamoussoukro (Cote d'Ivoire) and Madrid (Spain) – assistance from Okayama (Japan).
- The sub-region R99 will have the capitals in Ouagadougou (Burkina Faso) and London (United Kingdom) - assistance from Vaasa (Finland).

London, from the Shard (2012, 309 m, observatory at 244 m, floors 68 to 72, floor area 758 m^2), at 72nd floor, outside in fresh air, looking at the top and the internal structure of the building's spire (65 m) and radiator floors from 73rd to 95th. Under the observatory there are 13 floors for residences, with a total of 5,772 m^2. The highest point is 309.7 m, and the steelwork highest point is 308.5 m. The Shard is the tallest building in the European Union.

Question 12. Around 1110 BC, was Babylonia involved in helping when disagreement appears at the Level 3 Management?

Response 12: No, too busy with errors - around 1110 BC Babylonia had a war with Elam, southeast neighbor.

The ten Level 3 friendly managers for the 10 regions will have plenty of disagreements, but they will harmoniously work, using calm and convincing arguments, to clarify the issues, and return to harmonious working environment.

Level 3 Management: Ten L3 friendly managers for the 10 regions, who will supervise and assist the 10 L2 managers of the 10 sub-regions of each region, for a total of about 770,000,000 people for each region.

- The Region R0 will have the first capitals in

Bern (Switzerland) and Libreville (Gabon) – assistance from Oxford (UK).

For better quality and consistency of the management, we'll have the first two cities from the region R0, and the third city from outside. Actually, being inside the same country Terra, any city, sub-region or region can ask for advice or help from anybody.

- The Region R1 will have the first capitals in

Warsaw (Poland) and Pretoria (South Africa) – assistance from Miami (FL, USA).

- The Region R2 will have the first capitals in

Moscow (Russia) and Cairo (Egypt) – assistance from Grenoble (France).

- The Region R3 will have the first capitals in

Astana (Kazakhstan) and Karachi (Pakistan), – assistance from Montpellier (France).

Italy, Venezia, Accademia di Belle Arti di Venezia (center-right) on Fondamenta Zattere allo Spirito Santo, on the north bank of Canale della Giudecca..

- The Region R4 will have the first capitals in

New Delhi (India) and Novosibirsk (Russia) - assistance from Magdeburg (Germany).

- The Region R5 will have the first capitals in

Krasnoyarsk (Russia) and Urumqi (China) - assistance from Avignon (France).

- The Region R6 will have the first capitals in

Jakarta (Indonesia) and Beijing (China) - assistance from Neuchâtel (Switzerland).

- The Region R7 will have the first capitals in

Tokyo (Japan) and Sydney (Australia) - assistance from Malmö (Sweden).

- The Region R8 will have the first capitals in

Washington (USA) and Mexico City (Mexico) - assistance from Bellinzona (Switzerland).

- The Region R9 will have the first capitals in

Halifax (Canada) and Brasilia (Brazil) - assistance from Biel (Switzerland).

Italy, Gate 2 to the ruins of Pompeii (650 BC, in 79 covered by ash), with a panel entitled FACTA NON VERBA (deeds, not words), a Latin famous phrase. Pompeii was an ancient Roman town, with a big water system, amphitheater, gymnasium and a port, 20 km southeast of Naples, 10 km southeast of Mt. Vesuvius.

Question 13. Around 1046 BC, on the Yellow River in China, was harmony connected to the Level 4 Management?

Response 13: No, because of the many errors - around 1046 BC the Zhou rebel forces had a war with Shang Dynasty, in the middle and lower of Yellow River valley in China.

The harmony is a precious human value, reflecting compatibility and accord in many areas, like feelings, actions, relationships, opinions and interests – exactly what is needed for a good advanced civilization.

Level 4 very friendly 10 Advisers of the world, who will supervise and assist the 10 L3 managers of the 10 regions of the Earth, for a total of about 7,700,000,000 people – all the people on Earth, citizens of Peaceful Terra.

Japan, Nagoya: a tall building seen from Shinkansen (the bullet train, 320 km/h, started in 1964),

Question 14. In 854 BC, in Mesopotamia, are they thinking where will the 10 Advisors be located?

Response 14: No, too busy with errors - for about 8 years, between 854 BC and 846 BC, the Assyrian Empire (in Mesopotamia) had a war of conquest of Aram (now Syria and around).

Harmony means a state of balance among different ideas, with the purpose of advancing and getting better.

The L4 very friendly 10 Advisers of the world will be located each in one the ten Regions R0, R1,..., R9. For example, in the beginning, for the first month (then changing every month), the ten Advisers of the world will be located:

- in R0: Barcelona (Spain)
- in R1: Benghazi (Libya)
- in R2: Addis Ababa (Ethiopia)
- in R3: Hyderabad (Pakistan)
- in R4: Bhopal (India)
- in R5: Mandalay (Myanmar)
- in R6: Nanchong (China)
- in R7: Khabarovsk (Russia)
- in R8: Houston (USA)
- in R9: Recife (Brazil)

These ten L4 Advisers will be in permanent contact with each other, and with the L3 Advisers, for the best management of the world.

The ten L4 Advisers will move each month from a first capital of a region to the second capital of another region, at random (or based on urgency, if an emergency occurred). This mobility is essential for having a long period of tranquility and harmony.

The Advisors will be located in the current government buildings, and the excess government buildings and properties will be sold, in order to increase the budget, and to reduce the expenses.

The top 10 Advisers (and all the others) will collaborate via e-mail, telephone, videoconferences, mail, or face to face, when needed, to produce practical results for all people, very fast.

USA, Washington (1790), National Archives and Records Administration building (1935), on Constitution Avenue.

Question 15. In 740 BC, in Sparta, were they analyzing how will harmony help the 10 Advisors to take decisions?

Response 15: Noy yet, too many errors - for 20 years, between 740 BC and 720 BC, Sparta (south of Greece) was at war with Messenia – its western neighbor, called first Messenian war.

Harmony is a sine qua non requirement for good management, because all the decisions will be by consensus only.

It is expected that the 10 Advisors are talented enough to be able to negotiate fast any disagreements between them, and quickly arrive at the best common decision, for the benefit of all people.

Japan, Mount Fuji (Fuji-san, 3776 m), seen from Fujiyoshida, circa 15 km north-est from Mount Fuji, 1000 m altitude.

Question 16. Were elections contemplated in 722 BC in China?

Response 16: Not yet, unfortunately - for 241 years, between 722 BC and 481 BC, there were continuous wars of the Chinese Spring and Autumn period.

Living in peace and harmony with ourselves an all the people around means living and working together peacefully, for the benefit of all.

The ten L4 Advisers will be elected from the 10 regions, and each of them will be the First Adviser (***First among equals*** – from Latin: Primus inter pares) for one month, by rotation.

The First Adviser only coordinates the work of the other 9 Advisors for one month.

Finland, Helsinki: the Railway Square, east of the railway station, with the Finnish National Theatre (1872 - 1902, back) and the statue of Aleksis Kivi (1834 – 1872, aged 38, the first Finnish novelist).

Question 17. Any thinking on how to inform the people in 685 BC in Sparta?

Response 17: Not yet - for 17 years, between 685 BC and 668 BC, Sparta was again at war with its western neighbor Messenia – the second Messenian war.

To maintain a peaceful and harmonious atmosphere for all people, the 10 Advisers will be using a Monthly World Report.

The First Adviser, on the last day of each month, will present in writing for the world (no more than 5 standard pages) a clear and precise Monthly World Report, with a list of finished and unfinished tasks.

The other 9 Advisers will add their comments to the Monthly World Report (no more than half a page each - total report less than 9.5 pages).

In order to better know the world government, to help it, and, especially, to improve it, all able people of the world will work as volunteers at least one day per year in each of the seven departments.

After each Monthly World Report, a public opinion survey about the report should be taken, and presented to all Advisors.

All activities of the Advisors, and others from the small World Government, will be available to the people on a website.

France, Paris: Sculpture on the right side of the entrance to Palais de la Découverte (1937, the west wing of the Grand Palais, 1900, on Avenue Franklin Delano Roosevelt), with a science museum, presenting interactive science and astronomy exhibits. Jean Baptiste Perrin (1870-1942, French physicist), winner of the 1926 Nobel Prize in Physics, created this science museum dedicated to scientific discovery, showing various experiments in astronomy, chemistry, earth science, life science, physics and mathematics.

Question 18. Any management responsibilities explained in 642 BC in Rome?

Response 18: Not yet - for 304 years, between 642 BC and 338 BC, the Romans were at war with the Latins (the early inhabitants of the city of Rome and around).

Harmony has a high priority for all Advisers.

The top 10 Advisers will manage Police and all other Departments.

For obvious uncooperative or improper attitude of one top Advisor X, the other 9 can replace X with X's number 2, and X will receive appropriate medical treatment.

When vacancies happen for Advisors, the number 2 for those Advisors will fill the vacancies.

All the activities of all Advisors will be recorded in computers and videos, and on paper, for people to be able to see what they are doing.

Advisors at all levels should work 40 hours/week, with 4 weeks of vacation, but many services (medical, police (firemen should be part of the police), emergency, volunteers) should be non-stop.

Advisors' compensation should be the world annual average salary (in 2019 less than $10,000) plus 4% of that world average salary, for level 4 (total $10,400), + 3 % for level 3, and so on. They all should work to increase the world average salary, in order to get themselves an increase.

All the other world government employees will have a compensation close to the average compensation of the people in the area where they are located.

All Advisors are free to speak about their administrative work, with modesty.

At least 7 of the top 10 Advisers should be present every working day.

USA, Boston (founded in 1630): on a visiting tall ship, at the Boston Fish Pier (opened in 1915).

Question 19. Is harmony excluding war in 595 BC in Greece?

Response 19: No - for 10 years, between 595 BC and 585 BC, there was the first sacred war, between the Amphictyonic League of Delphi (cities around Delphi, Central Greece) and Kirha (harbor of Delphi).

Advisors (and all the others) cannot declare war, reprisals or capture land or water.

Advisors (and all the others) cannot raise and support armies, navy, or any military forces.

Japan, 13 km north-east from Mount Fuji, the easternmost and largest of the five lakes, Lake Yamanaka is also the third highest lake in Japan, standing at 980 meters above sea level.

Question 20. In 552 BC, in Persia, who will harmoniously help the management?

Response 20: Regrettably, nobody - for 13 years, between 552 BC and 539 BC, Cyrus of Persia had wars and occupied many neighbors.

Each Advisor, and each manager at all levels, will have 5 immediate assistants, who will harmoniously work together for the benefit of all people.

Each Advisor, and each manager at all levels, will have 5 immediate assistants:
1) a mathematician for finance and all other calculations,
2) a medical doctor for keeping everybody healthy, calm, polite, friendly and optimist,
3) a CEO for good management,
4) an engineer for all practical projects, and
5) a teacher for education, training and related areas.

The five assistants play a key role, because they are highly qualified professionals, who actually will carry on the practical management of the world.

The five assistants' integrity, professionalism and friendliness will significantly improve the quality of the world and local governments.

The five assistants are really the experts. They will assist the Advisors and all levels of management, in order to have an efficient, correct and professional working of the world government at all levels.

All spending proposals from Advisers must be approved by their 5 assistants (doctors, mathematicians, CEOs, engineers and teachers), and must have an already existing funding in the budget.

Finland, Helsinki: The Railway Square, east of the railway station, with the Finnish National Theatre (1872 - 1902, left).

UK, London, from the northwest side of the Tower of London (left up), looking southeast to the three western external walls, 180 m from the Tower.

Question 21. In 499 BC, in Sparta, who will oversee the top management?

Response 21: Well, nobody - for 51 years, between 499 BC and 448 BC, Athens, Sparta and other Greek cities had wars with Persia and its allies.

Understanding other people is a generator of harmony and peace.

An Honorific World Observer will be quietly elected by direct vote – starting, for example, 1st September 2022 - for only one 3 years term, with the main duty to observe that the top 10 Advisers efficiently perform their duties, and keep their words – if they don't, they will be changed.

For managers and for everybody else, keeping their word is a serious and strict requirement.

The Honorific World Observer has this responsibility for the top 10 Advisors, but all people will pay attention to this. Words must become again important and respected.

Question 22. In 475 BC, in China, are they thinking about clarity and harmony for the World Government?

Response 22: Not yet, too busy with making errors - for 254 years, between 475 BC and 221 BC, there were many wars of the warring states period in China.

Clarity and harmony are the foundation of the World Government, because the communication with people is based on this foundation.

All the employees of the World Government are temporary, and must reapply for their positions every year.

There is no need for unions.

The World Government will be limited to:
1) the Office of the Honorific Observer (less than 10 employees),
2) the Office of the top ten Advisors (less than 100 employees), and
3) 7 small departments.

Question 23. In 431 BC, in Peloponnesus, are they listening to Hippocrates, and working on the 7 World Government Departments?

Response 23: Not yet, too busy making mistakes - for 27 years, between 431 BC and 404 BC, the Peloponnesian War took place, between Peloponnesian League (Sparta and other cities from Peloponnesus, south of Greece) and Delian League (Athens and other cities around).

It is important to note that the famous Greek physician Hippocrates was born around 460 BC in Kos, Greece, and died around 370 BC in Larissa, Greece, aged circa 90. He said:

"Wherever the art of medicine is loved, there is also a love of humanity."

The World Government will have these 7 small departments:

- Tax Department

- Collects taxes of 15% of the income of people and revenue of companies.

- The Manager of the Tax Department is appointed for a three-year term by the World 10 Advisers.

- The number of employees must be under 50,000, with excellent computers, and advanced software.

France, Paris: The north-west side of Tour Eiffel (1889, 324 m, 279 m at the 3rd level), Pont d'Iéna over Seine (center down, 1808-1814, by Napoleon, 155 m by 35 m), Av de New York (before the bridge, on the north side of la Seine), Jardin du Trocadéro (down, 1878, 1937, with the Fountain of Warsaw), looking south-east from the Esplanade du Trocadéro (the terrace between the south-west (left) and north-east (right) façades of Palais de Chaillot (1937)).

- Treasury

Treasury will control all the financial issues, including:
- antitrust
- fiscal service
- financial cooperation
- financing bank
- world reserve system
- world budget using only revenue, no borrowing, and spending only on strict necessary needs
– all the budgets, at all levels, will have a 2% surplus, which will be returned to the taxpayers
- register of all government papers and activities
- archives and records
- assist all people to have savings accounts for old age (the old age will be starting around 70), and 10% of their income should automatically go to their savings accounts. For those unable to work, their doctors and mathematicians will decide case by case.
- bankruptcies, in general, will be discouraged, and when strict necessary, will be analyzed and solved, case by case, by the doctors, mathematicians and CEOs who worked with the people who asked the bankruptcy.
- encourage all families to assist their parents, grandparents, and great-grandparents.
- housing finance
- housing for all people
- no homelessness
- consumer financial protection
- pensions
- privacy
- current social security until replaced by personal savings
- personnel management
- general services for the world government
- each the 10 regions will receive 2.5% of the world taxes - at least 30% of the money will be sent to villages and cities.
- each of the 100 sub-regions will receive 0.25% of the world taxes. At least 40% of the money will be sent to villages and cities.

- The World Central Bank will include all current central banks – starting, for example, on May 1st, 2023.
- The Special Credit Card (SCC) will be issued by the World Central Bank.
- Advisors will create a new world currency, named, for example, "coin", and all the other currencies will be exchanged for coins. The World Central Bank will implement the details.
- The counterfeiting and all other bad things, which some sick people do, will be medically treated (in specialized medical institutions when necessary), and those who did bad things will pay all the expenses, and will reimburse the victims. Victims will always be very protected, and helped to recover the losses from the attackers.

France, Paris: The main entrance on the east façade of the Grand Palais des Champs-Élysées (1900), on Avenue Winston Churchill.

- People Assistance Department

It will assist people in general, including:
- parent assistance
- dispute resolution
- in very simple disputes or culpa levis (ordinary negligence, like late payments, etc.), one single assistant will decide within minutes, and all people will go back to work
- census every 5 years
- election assistance every 20 months
- special credit cards
- people protection against abuses from anybody
- completely eliminate corruption, organized crime and drug trafficking
- all people in the world will remain in their places, and the improvements will come to them. Those who want to move to other places, will need first a special invitation from at least 10 people (not family related) where they want to move.
- all the Tribunals and related areas will be transformed in people assistance services, based on friendliness, collaboration and goodwill.
- It is well understood that no excessive bail will be required, no excessive fines imposed, no cruel and unusual punishments applied, but, at the same time, it is well understood that a person who did a bad thing will receive the necessary corrective medical treatment, and will reimburse all people who suffered damages, and the medical treatment. The victims will always receive special attention.
- Nobility (King, Prince, etc.) could continue to exist in some places, but they should not interfere with activities of the Advisors, and actually should help them.
- food safety
- trash & recycling
- free commerce
- jobs assistance
- postal service
- labor safety and harmonious relations
- land, water

- volunteers
- because late payments are very frequent sources of conflict, the world government will have sufficient people to solve these small issues promptly, for a small fee (like 1% of the amount).
- fitness, sport, tourism
- 10 world holidays: the normal 4 Earth events (2 solstices (around 21 June, around 21 December), and 2 equinoxes (around 21 March, around 21 September), Mother's Day on 1st May, Father's Day on 6 August, Children's Day on 6 November, Grandparents' Day on 6 February, and 2 optional days (like Thanksgiving or a Religious Day (Christmas), and New Year).

Finland, Helsinki Central railway station (1907 – 1914), on Brunnsgatan, in the city center.

- Medical Department

It will manage all medical and healthcare related areas, including:
- human services
- conflict resolution
- families, children, elderly
- medicine approval
- disease control and prevention
- medical doctors and assistants will make regular home visits, at least once a year, to all people, to keep them healthy, and to prevent illnesses.
- medical research: cancer, heart, lung, blood, arthritis, surgical robotics, connected computers for healthcare, etc.
- healthy homes, streets, stores, working places, etc.
- healthy aging
- all misunderstandings, disagreements or conflicts of any nature will be treated by medical personnel (with police help when strict necessary), until all is back to normal.
- no prisons are necessary, only specialized medical institutions (in simple cases, the places where the treated people live can be used, with the necessary limitations and surveillance)
- If a person X is considered that did a bad thing, X will have, within 3 days, a discussion with one or more doctors and other assistants, and will be informed of the nature and cause of the bad thing; including witnesses against and for him. Then a decision will be taken within other 3 days, by a group of doctors and other assistants. Victims of bad people will always have priority to discuss their problems with one or more doctors and other assistants, and quick decisions will be taken within 3 days, by a group of doctors and other assistants. Protection of victims has always priority.
- in order to better know the world government, to help it, and, especially, to improve it, all able people of the world will work as volunteers at least one day per year in the local facility of this department, which will have a special office for managing this volunteer work.

– all people will have government medical insurance, and they can also have private medical insurance
– there will be doctors working for the government 100%, or only part-time, or having only private practice, all with reasonable salaries and fees.
– there will be government pharmaceutical institutions and private pharmaceutical companies, offering reasonable priced medicines, without advertising to the general public.

USA, Washington (1790), National Gallery of Art (1937, National Mall).

France, Paris: A statue at the south-west corner of Palais de la Découverte (the west building of the Grand Palais, 1900, on Avenue Franklin Delano Roosevelt), with a science museum, presenting interactive science and astronomy exhibits. The Grand Palais des Champs-Élysées is a monument dedicated by the Republic to the glory of French art, 240 m long, constructed with an iron, steel and glass barrel-vaulted roof, the last of the large transparent structures.

- Police

Police will provide assistance for:

- accidents
- disasters
- complete elimination of nuclear, chemical and biological arms, firearms and explosives
- world complete security
- world cooperation
- conflict reduction and resolution
- investigations
- emergency assistance
- training
- delinquency prevention in general, and especially juvenile
- protection of Advisors, important government buildings, etc.
- extended surveillance and reconnaissance to prevent bad events
- fire protection
- volunteers to help police
- police will be present at public meetings, services, shows, etc., in order to protect the public
- public order
- ensuring traffic safety
- completely eliminate corruption, organized crime and drug trafficking
- movement of people based on civilized rules
- assist and protect those who have encountered violence
- World Police and specialists from the former United Nations and Interpol will be ready and very mobile for urgent and special operations, when they are needed.
- Police will be the only department which will have some small arms, in order to stop some very bad people (who are very sick).
- a small manufacturing and maintenance of arms unit will be part of the Police Department, under strict control.
- Police will work with medical personnel, mathematicians, CEOs, engineers, teachers and others, to make sure that all the people on the Planet are in good mental health, in order to prevent bad situations. This is also a major responsibility of all Advisors.

- prevention of bad events
- The Advisors will allocate the necessary budget for Police, and Police will assist people in need.

Japan, 13 km north-east from Mount Fuji, the easternmost and largest of the five lakes, Lake Yamanaka is also the third highest lake in Japan, standing at 980 meters above sea level.

- Education Department

- Over 2 billions of children in the world will get a solid peace-oriented education, to give a solid peace-oriented foundation for a good, free, peaceful and prosperous life.
- Education is very important – teachers will work with parents and grandparents, to educate the children to leave healthy in a sustainable peace, liberty and prosperity.
- Discipline must be strict, and those who do not behave properly, will get medical assistance.
- The world will have 4 school levels (SLs) of education:

SL1 – Kindergarten – 2 years: age 5 and 6
SL2 – Primary School – 4 years: age 7, 8, 9 and 10
SL3 – Secondary School – 3 years: age 11, 12 and 13
SL4 – High School or Vocational School – 4 years: age 14, 15, 16 and 17

- A World Library will include the Library of Congress and all the other great libraries – they will remain where they are now, but will be digitally interconnected, and accessible from any place in the world.
- adult education: technical, career
- training for employment
- management training
- post high school education
- peace education
- world constitution education

Italy, Rome (753 BC, one of the oldest cities in Europe, called Roma Aeterna (The Eternal City) and Caput Mundi (Capital of the World)), from the Pincian Hill looking southwest: Piazza del Popolo (1822), with the Egyptian obelisk (36 m) of Sety I (1290–1279 BC) and Rameses II (1303, 1279–1213 BC) from Heliopolis, brought in 10 BC by Augustus (63 BC-14 AD) for Circus Maximus, in 1589 here. Basilica San Pietro (1506, 132 m, back).

- Science & Technology Department.

It will help in the areas of:
- mathematics
- statistics
- science
- technology
- Algorithmic Governance will be an essential tool for a better and impartial governing of the world, used by the Advisers elected by people. Mathematicians from all countries will work to improve the Algorithmic Governance, to better serve the people.
- cyberspace complete security will be achieved and strictly maintained
- information systems
- computer services
- Internet
- scientific cooperation
- economic development at the world level
- infrastructure improvement and maintenance at the world level
- innovation and improvements in all areas, at the world level
- transportation at the world level
- safety
- security
- aviation
- highway
- cars
- railroads without noise
- maritime administration
- logistics
- strategic planning at the world level
- public works
- fleet maintenance
- standards: weights, measures, etc.
- research at the world level
- risk analysis
- laboratories
- engineering

- communications at the world level
- telecommunications
- networks
- peaceful nuclear energy use at the world level
- safety
- waste
- electrical power
- oceanic analysis at the world level
- atmospheric analysis at the global level
- meteorological service and prognosis at the global level
- world resources analysis
- sustainable use of world resources
- geographical and geological activity
- product safety at the global level
- hazardous material and chemical safety
- government broadcasting (radio, tv, Internet, newspaper, etc.) including news, scientific and technical information
- private broadcasting will continue, but the world government must be able to directly inform the people, without intermediaries
- space exploration and expansion at the world level – very important for the future
- patent and trademark
- intellectual rights
- all government work, which can be done by private companies, will be contracted with the best and reasonably priced private companies. At the same time, the government should always have competitive services for people – from plumbing and electrical help, to mortgage and buying or selling a house.

Question 24. In 410 BC, in Sicily, were they working on the frequency of harmonious elections?

Response 24: No, just errors after errors - for 70 years, between 410 BC and 340 BC, Syracuse (Sicily), Corinth and Sparta had wars with Athens, Delian League and Segesta (Sicily), called the Second Sicilian War.

The Advisers should be elected every 20 months for one term only. If an Adviser X was elected for a term T1, then the next term T2 will have another Advisor Y. For the next term T3, X can be elected again, but the next term T4 will have a new Adviser, and so on. All levels of Advisers (minimum age 25 years) can be elected, not consecutively, at most 4 times (maximum 80 months = 6 years and 8 months).

All the employees in Government will respect Seneca's (circa 1,960 years ago) aphorism "To govern is to serve, not to rule", and Hippocrates' (over 2,400 years ago) aphorism "Make a habit of two things: to help; or at least to do no harm."

Advisers should have exceptional results obtained from their work, and based on these results, plus modesty, moderation, good character, friendliness, sharp mind, wisdom, good morals, and intense desire to help people, they will be elected, without any campaigning, publicity, fundraising, donations, debates, propaganda, political parties, advertising, or similar activities.

There will be use of advanced digital technology, which opens up entirely new opportunities for developing direct elections, and public control of the institutions, improving the transparency of the election procedure, and taking into account the interests and opinions of each voter (over the age of 21, who are not in a special medical institution for bad behavior or for mental health).

France, Paris: The statue “Flore” (1937) by Marcel Gimond (1894 – 1961, French sculptor, studied at the Beaux-Arts Academy in Lyon, and then he was the student in turn of both Aristide Maillol (1861 – 1944) and Auguste Rodin (1840 – 1917)), on the south-west façade of Palais de Chaillot (1937, named after a former village which was here, with architectural, naval and ethnographic museums), on the hill of the Trocadéro.

Question 25. In 395 BC, in Corinth, Greece, were they seriously checking the qualifications of the leaders?

Response 25: Not at all, too many errors left and right - for 8 years, between 395 BC and 387 BC, there was the Corinthian War between Athens, Argos, Corinth, Thebes and others, and Sparta with the Peloponnesian League.

An Election Commission of 110 representatives from the 10 regions and from the 100 sub-regions, elected separately for 5 years, will have to examine the qualifications of all the candidates for Advisers, and for other senior management positions. Unqualified candidates will be asked to improve their qualifications, and then to try again later.

It is important to refresh the management, and to bring new people to help the big family of 7.7 B people. The older generations, who performed well, will be retained in important roles, because experience and maturity count very much. At least two months before the retirement, they will kindly be asked to transfer their expertise to the younger generation. Even after retirement, they will occasionally be invited to share their expertise.

In every election, with every winner, will be other two for number 2 and number 3. The number 2 and number 3 for each management position will be used when number 1 is not available (vacation, sick, etc.). They will constantly work for number 1, helping to solve urgent problems for the people.

Good elections are essential for the future.

There has been a tendency to make elections conflict generating events, with lots of propaganda, false information, heavy donations, unpolite confrontations, bully fundraising, hostile political parties and organizations, unlimited power ambitions, etc.

This will be completely changed into clean, friendly elections, in which people choose between leaders with outstanding results, plus talent to lead people to peace and freedom, modesty, moderation, good character, friendliness, sharp mind, wisdom, good morals, and intense desire to help people – no campaigning, no publicity, no fundraising, no donations, no debates, no propaganda, no political parties, no advertising, or similar activities.

All Advisors should also be local Administrators – they must show that they are good managers, and produce practical results for all people.

Italy, Venezia, Palazzo Dandolo on Riva degli Schiavoni, 150 m east of Piazza San Marco.

Question 26. In 334 BC, was Alexander from Macedon consulting the people?

Response: Unfortunately, no, he was just doing the usual errors of the young rulers (he died at the age of 32.9 in Babylon – he, 23 years old, told Diogenes, 79, "If I were not Alexander, I should wish to be Diogenes", but Diogenes (412 BC – 323 BC, aged 89, 56 years older than Alexander, they died in the same year, Greek philosopher) responded "If I were not Diogenes, I should wish to be Diogenes". Diogenes also said: "The foundation of every state is the education of its youth." "The mob is the mother of tyrants.") - for 11 years, between 334 BC and 323 BC, there were the wars of Alexander from Macedon against Greek city states, Persian Empire and others.

An electronic world referendum will be organized every three months. The main questions will be:

1. Are you satisfied with the Government?
2. What Government work is good?
3. What Government work is not good?
4: Suggestions for improvement:

Within two months after each referendum, the Government will respond to the people. Based on the suggestions received, new pro-people rules will be replacing some old rules.

From Westminster Bridge Road looking west to the bridge with the railroads going to Waterloo Station (to right), and to new original buildings on Westminster Bridge Road at Lambeth Palace Road, south of the Park Plaza Westminster Bridge London Hotel (to right), 400 m east from the Westminster Bridge ((1862, 250 m, width 26 m, 7 spans), 600 m southeast from the London Eye (2000), and 500 m south from the Waterloo Station (1922, 24 platforms, railway terminus, and underground, in Lambeth).

Question 27. In 321 BC, in India, were they thinking to eliminate arms?

Response: Not at all - from 321 BC to 320 BC, Maurya Empire (central and north India) occupied its neighbor Nanda Empire (north-east India).

Arms will not exist anymore, and only the police will have some small arms. Those who want arms for hunting or sport, will borrow them from police stations, with proper documents, rules and payments.

All military units will become strong civilian organizations, working to improve the quality of life for everybody.

For practical reasons, the transition from the current imperfect situation to the much better Sustainable Peace and Prosperity Structure (SPPS) will be very smooth: first - all the countries remain as they are, and they will begin – for example on January 1st, 2022 - to negotiate total and complete disarmament, with the help of the United Nations, for 3 months. Then for 5 months will intensely work to eliminate all the arms – either transform them in peaceful tools, or destroy them. Then a continuous verification and monitoring will be implemented, the make sure that the world finally achieved complete disarmament forever!

Question 28. Was census on the minds of the rulers in 280 BC in Rome?

Response: No, too busy with mistakes - for 5 years, between 280 BC and 275 BC, there was the Pyrrhic War, between the Roman Republic with Carthage (now in Tunisia), and Magna Graecia (south of Italy), Epirus (now Albania) and Samnium (south-east Italy).

A census will take place every 5 years – starting, for example, on October 1st, 2023 - and all people will receive a special credit card (SCC), with their photo and other personal data. The delimitations between regions, and between sub-regions, will be adjusted by the census.

Italy, Cividale del Friuli: 3 Nov 2009, on Corso Paolino d'Aquileia, on the bridge of Iacopo da Bissone (1442, 50 m by 3.6 m, height 22.5 m, rock) over Natisone River (flowing from back to front), 150 m southeast of Palazzo Comunale, looking northeast to il Campanile of Monastero Santa Maria in Valle (650, up left) and Natisone River.

Question 29. In 274 BC, in Egypt, any thinking about having some helping card cards?

Response: No, just the same old war errors - for 74 years, between 274 BC and 200 BC, there were 5 Syrian Wars – the Ptolemaic Kingdom (Egypt under Greek rulers, started by a friend of Alexander) attacked Seleucid Empire (Syria and around, under Greek rulers, started by another friend of Alexander).

The special credit card (SCC) will be used to buy everything, to identify for voting, for census, for travel, for medical assistance, etc.

The current private credit cards will continue to work as usual.

The changes of the delimitations between regions, and also sub-regions, will be inputted on these cards, and no other work is needed.

Question 30. Who are sacred for people in 264 BC, in Rome?

Response: Nobody, unfortunately, all are immersed in war errors - for 118 years, between 264 BC and 146 BC, there were 3 Punic Wars – the Roman Republic attacked Carthage (north of Tunisia). Only 2,131 years later, in 1985, a ceremonial peace was signed.

People are something sacred for people

The enemies of the people on Earth are not other people, but viruses, microbes, bad bacteria and hundreds of deadly illnesses – all people on Earth will work together, in a harmonious effort, against these real enemies for all of us.

Italy, Rome (753 BC), from cordonata capitolina (flight of steps, which can be also used by horses, with balustrades ending down with two Egyptian lions in black basalt, and up with two marble statues of Castor (left) and Pollux (right), by Michelangelo), Campidoglio (1546 by Michelangelo, on Collis Capitolinus, the oldest part of Rome, with Temple of Jupiter, 509 BC), Palazzo Senatorio (back, 1350, atop Tabularium, now the city hall).

Question 31. Any non-violence and harmony ideas in 230 BC, in China?

Response: Regrettably, not yet - for 9 years, from 230 BC to 221 BC, Qin had many wars against 6 of his neighbors in China.

Very clearly, we need harmonious relationships between all people.

Non-violence is a strict requirement for all activities on Earth.

The first rule for everybody on Earth comes from the Hippocratic Oath: Primum non nocere - first do not harm, mentioned over 2,400 years ago.

Question 32. In 215 BC, in Rome, were they thinking about the importance of the doctors?

Response: Very sadly, no, war errors were everywhere - for 47 years, between 215 BC and 168 BC, the Roman Republic had wars against Macedonian Empire (north of Greece and Persia).

Home visits will be the real joy, and will be full of harmony.

Medical doctors and assistants will make regular home visits to all people, to keep them healthy, and to prevent illnesses.

Italy, Rome (753 BC), on Via dei Fori Imperiali (for pedestrians only on holidays), Amphitheatrum Flavium (80, called Colosseum, back), Basilica of Maxentius and Constantine (312, right).

Question 33. Anyone thinking about the truth in 209 BC, in Parthian Empire?

Response: Sadly, no, the truth is a perpetual problem, because the first casualty in wars and conflicts is the truth - for 121 years, between 209 BC and 88 BC, the Parthian Empire (now Iran) had many wars with the Seleucid Empire (near Iran, under Greek rulers, started by a friend of Alexander).

Harmony also means to have similar goals, therefore the truth is always needed!

People need only truth in order to create a long term peaceful and harmonious society.

If someone lies – medical treatment will follow.

Italy, Venezia, Università Ca' Foscari di Venezia, on Fondamenta di San Giobbe, at the north-west entrance of Canale di Cannaregio, on the north-west part of Venezia.

Ca' Foscari University of Venice was founded in 1868, as the first Italian business college.

The main seat of the University is Ca' Foscari Palace, the Venetian Gothic building placed in the largest bend of the Grand Canal. The palace was purchased and renewed by Doge Francesco Foscari in 1452. It contains important artistic and architectural works, such as: a room with a 15th century frescoed floor and a 16th century decorated roof; a room with a 16th century stucco work by the Venetian sculpture Alessandro Vittoria (1525-1608); a great hall designed by the Venetian architect Carlo Scarpa (1906-1978), with two murals by Mario Sironi and Mario de Luigi.

Ca' Foscari participates actively in the city's cultural life, organizing over 400 events every year. The University holds successful art exhibitions in "Ca' Foscari Esposizioni", the exhibition space in the main building. Ca' Foscari also offers nine Summer Schools including the prestigious Ca' Foscari - Harvard Summer School, the result of a bilateral agreement between Ca' Foscari and the American university.

Question 34. Any idea about freedom in 162 BC, in central Asia?

Response: No, only errors of war and invasions - for 92 years, between 162 BC and 70 BC, nomadic people from central Asia repeatedly invaded the Greco-Bactrian Kingdom (now north of Afghanistan, under Greek rulers, starting from friends of Alexander).

It is fundamental for all people – freedom and harmony go hand in hand, you cannot have harmony without freedom.

Freedom is a fundamental requirement on Earth.

It is well understood that this freedom refers to doing good things in a civilized manner, not for war, violence or similar bad things, which are against the wellbeing of the people.

Freedom goes hand in hand with responsibility.

People can assemble peacefully only.

Question 35. What about the economy, in 133 BC, in China?

Response: Some economy existed, and people wanted to work for a better life, but the errors of war, bureaucracy, and no freedom stopped their efforts - for 44 years, between 133 BC and 89 BC, Han Empire (east and south China) had wars against Xiongnu (north of China).

For economy it is clear that the free market economy, while not perfect, gives the best results, but all people will have the option to choose between friendly private services, and friendly government services. Independent assistants and monitors will make sure that there are no abuses. Sine qua non requirements for happiness are morality and free market.

Italy, Venezia, Rio Ca' Foscari (left), Palazzo Balbi (center), left bank, 2.2 km from Ponte degli Scalzi

Question 36. What about religion in 66 BC in Rome?

Response: Religion has a continuous presence from the very beginning of civilization, and unfortunately, was used by many rulers to justify their war errors - for 283 years, between 66 BC and 217 AD, the Romans had wars with the Parthian Empire (now Iran plus parts of its neighbors).

Religion will be free, and will help people, because usually religion promotes harmony.

The religion should be free, and is expected not to interfere with activities of the Advisors, and actually should help people.

Finland, Helsinki: a Baltic Sea canal from west to east, near Ruoholahdenpuisto, seen from a bridge on Bottenhavsgatan, near Helsinki Conservatory of Music (left).

Question 37. Could people petition the Government in 6 AD, in Korea?

Response: There were some rudimentary methods of petitioning the government, with very poor results, because of the errors of war - for 15 years, between 6 and 21, Goguryeo (north and central Korea kingdom) had wars and occupied Dongbuyeo (northeast Korea kingdom).

People of course can petition the small Word Government, and can change it anytime, if it does not perform as expected.

Italy, the entrance to the modern city of Pompei, located southeast of the ruins of the ancient Pompeii (650 BC, in 79 covered by ash).

Question 38. Was spending less than the revenue in 43 AD, in Rome?

Response: Generall, no, because of the errors with wars, but, occasionally, some better rulers had a more balanced budget - for 53 years, between 43 and 96, the Roman Empire occupied the British tribes.

If there is deficit, the harmony disappears:

All budgets will have a surplus of 2% - there will be a strict application of the Latin aphorism: "Sumptus censum ne superset" (Let not your spending exceed your income). As we can see, there were good Romans telling the rulers sumptus censum ne superset, but the rulers continued to make plenty of mistakes with wars, conflicts, etc.

On Newington Butts St., looking northwest to Metropolitan Tabernacle (1650, left) and London College of Communication.

Question 39. Any desire to eliminate old and new errors in 101, in Rome?

Response: No, just more war errors - between 101 and 106, Trajan from The Roman Empire had 2 Dacian wars, and occupied Dacian Kingdom (now Romania).

Correcting errors is a permanent duty for everybody - Darwin (over 140 years ago, around 1880) said "To kill an error is as good a service as, and sometimes even better than, the establishing of a new truth or fact."

Italy, Rome (753 BC), Forum Romanum, the northwest side of the white marble Arcus Septimii Severi (203 for the Parthian victories, Septimius Severus (born 145, Emperor 193–211, after Roman Emperor Julianus Didius (born 133, Emperor 193 (63 days))).

Question 40. Did they think of Seneca and kindness in 194, in China?

Response: No, the rulers just repeated the same war mistakes - for 5 years, 194 – 199, Sun Ce from the Eastern Hun dynasty of China had wars and occupied Shanyue (southern China and northern Vietnam).

Seneca (over 1,960 years ago, circa 4 BC – 65 AD, aged 69) said "Wherever there is a human being, there is an opportunity for a kindness."

This is a fundamental idea which must be constantly applied.

Italy, Rome: Accademia Nazionale dei Lincei (1603) in Villa Farnesina (1510). The author was invited to give a lecture here in 1977.

UK, Greenwich, on Gagarin (First Man in Space) Terrace, on the southwest part of the South Building (1899) of the Royal Observatory Greenwich (1676), looking northeast to the south part of the west side (right), the west part of the south side (left), and to the statue of Yuri Gagarin (1934-1968, Russian cosmonaut, the first man to journey into space, with Vostok spacecraft, which completed an orbit (1h 48') of the Earth on 12 April 1961. Resting place: Kremlin Wall Necropolis.

Question 41. Any idea of government mobility in 306, in Rome?

Response: No, just usual war errors - for 18 years, 306 – 324, Constantine I had wars with Maxentius, Licinius, Martinianus and others.

All levels of government will be highly mobile - changing of the capitals for the 10 regions, and for the 100 sub-regions, etc.

It is necessary to move the government close to the people, to be able to quickly solve the local problems.

Locally the people will decide how to better organize themselves, to be more efficient and harmonious, with the help of the world government when necessary. Like in any big family, there will be differences in organization and management, based on their abilities and objectives, but all must be peaceful and harmonious. Conflicts will be promptly resolved by the medical personnel, police, and other assistants.

Italy, Rome, COLVMNA·TRAIANI (113), commemorates Roman emperor Trajan's (53-117) victory in the Dacian Wars, constructed by Apollodorus of Damascus, located in Trajan's Forum, built near the Quirinal Hill, north of the Roman Forum; most famous for its spiral bas relief, which artistically describes the epic wars between the Romans and Dacians (101–102 and 105–106), 30 m in height, 35 m with pedestal, 20 colossal Carrara marble drums, each weighing about 32 tons, with a diameter of 3.7 m, 190-m frieze winds around the shaft 23 times, inside the shaft a spiral staircase of 185 steps provides access to a viewing platform at the top, the capital block of Trajan's Column weighs 53.3 tons.

Question 42. What about the World Police in 434 in Europe?

Response: Not such thing, just errors of war and invasions - for 19 years, 434 – 453, the first Hunnic Empire invaded Europe (Eastern Roman Empire, Western Roman Empire, Franks, Goths, Burgundians, Saxons, Alans, Germanic and Gallic tribes).

The United Nations will change in 2-3 years (for example, by 2024) into World Police and Assistance Organization (WPAO), to help local police in case of big natural disasters or big accidents, and will report to the top 10 Advisers. They will be located in all capitals, and help the locals. When an emergency appears, they will quickly move to solve the emergency.

The police powers will be limited, and they will know and be friend with all the people in their jurisdiction – this is the key element of a civilized and peaceful Earth. If they notice a person with bad intentions, they immediately retain that person and call for a medical assistant (and other assistants, if necessary), to analyze and solve the issue very quickly.

Police will be people's friends everywhere, and they will always help people.

Prevention of bad events is the main objective of everybody. If a bad event occurs, the police and their assistants will eliminate the consequences, reestablish the normal situation, and determine why the bad event occurred, in order to improve their activity, and prevent such bad events in the future.

Private property cannot be taken for public use, without just compensation, decided by at least 5 assistants.

A person cannot deprive another person of life, liberty, or property, which, unfortunately, occurs very frequently in the world, and very much effort and energy will be allocated to prevent such bad events.

In order to prevent bad things, the police, doctors and their assistants will be in permanent contact with all the people, by visiting them, phone calls, e-mails, tele-videos, and mail, to keep everybody calm and happy.

France, Paris: L'église de la Madeleine (Magdalenae, or L'église Sainte-Marie-Madeleine, or La Madeleine, 1842), a Roman Catholic Church in the 8th arrondissement of Paris, designed by Napoleon in 1806.

Question 43. Any idea of the World Government non-stop working in 492, in France?

Response: No, just more war errors - for 16 years, 492 – 508, Franks (now in France) had wars with the Visigoths (southwestern France and the Iberian Peninsula).

About 66% of the people of the world are working at any moment. Therefore, non-stop working of all world government departments – especially medical, police, emergency, volunteers – will be carefully organized.

Italy, ruins of Pompeii (650 BC, in 79 covered by ash), southeast of Via Stabiana (left and right), REG I INS IV on the left, REG I INS III on the right, Vicolo del Menandro (straight).

Question 44. What about privacy in 494 around Iraq?

Response: No, only more war errors - for 40 years, 494 – 534, Taghlib (Arab tribe from Najd) had wars with Banu Bakr (Arab tribe from vicinity).

In order to have serious and constructive discussions and negotiations, they must be private.

Privacy and discipline are necessary for good government work.

The results will be public and preserved, but not the private discussions.

Question 45. Any thoughts of a polite Government in 537 in Maya (southern Mexico and Guatemala)?

Response: No, too busy with war errors - for 35 years, 537 – 572, Calakmul (Maya city in southern Mexico) had wars with Tikal (Maya city in Guatemala).

It is a strict requirement for the top management, and for all others, to be highly civilized, polite, courteous, harmonious and efficient.

Who wants to work for the world government must have good manners.

Harmony in the world starts from the harmony and good manners of the people in the world government.

Because all people on Earth want to live in harmony right now, it will be relatively easy to implement this in one good and civilized country. This may include having small, beautiful and commonly agreed fences around properties, because good fences make good neighbors, and also helps with more privacy.

Question 46. Ready to end conflicts in 555 in the Visigothic Kingdom (southwestern France)?

Response: Not at all, only more errors of wars and conflicts - for 69 years, 555 – 624, Visigothic Kingdom (southwestern France) had wars with Eastern Roman Empire in Spain, and occupied Spain.

The medical personnel and others will work diligently to make sure that disputes are resolved, and then a friendship is developed. Only in this way the situation will become stable.

People want peace, freedom, health, friendship and prosperity, therefore conflicts should be quickly resolved, and then the corrective medical treatment will include the transformation of hostility and aggressiveness into harmony and friendship.

Dispute resolution is not only Government's obligation, but it will be everybody's duty.

There will be professional assistance from medical personnel, police, people assistance specialists, volunteers, religious organizations, and many others, but the bottom line is that everybody must avoid disputes.

When there are different opinions, just stay calm, express your opinion, listen to others, and continue calm the discussion until a compromise is reached.

There is no need to spend much time and energy – let the people decide, and even if your idea is not temporarily accepted, there are chances that in the future you'll have more people agree with you.

Italy, Venezia, Murano: A beautiful Murano glass sculpture in Murano Square. Murano's glassmakers created crystalline glass, enameled glass (smalto), glass with threads of gold (aventurine), multicolored glass.

Question 47. Any thinking on how to harmoniously communicate with other people in 598 in Korea?

Response: No, only war mistakes - for 16 years, 598 – 614, Goguryeo (Korean kingdom) had wars with Sui Dynasty (eastern China).

As a single big, over 7.7 B family on Earth, all people must be able to communicate easily with each other.

For this reason, a common language and alphabet on Earth are needed. Because English is a de facto common language now, it will be taken as the basis of the world language, let's call it Mundo, which will be taught in all schools, and used in the world government. All the other languages will continue as secondary languages.

The same is true for the Latin alphabet, which will be used everywhere, with other alphabets as secondary.

The teachers will have a very significant role in implementing this idea.

UK, London, on St Thomas St, looking southeast to the Shard (2009-2012, at London Bridge, 309 m (the tallest building in European Union), observatory at 244 m (72nd floor, 758 m^2), 95 floors, 72 habitable floors, 110,000 m^2 (11 ha) floor area, 44 elevators, architect Renzo Piano (born 1937, inspired by the London spires depicted by Canaletto (1697-1768)), 11,000 panes of glass (with a total surface area of 56,000 m^2 (5.6 ha)), post-tensioned concrete and composite floors, load-bearing pillars, tapering shape (sway tolerance 40 cm).

Question 48. Any heavy thinking about the global wealth in 600 in Frankish Empire?

Response: Not at all, too busy with war errors - for 193 years, 600 – 793, Frankish Empire (France and around) had wars with Frisian Kingdom (north of France).

The 2018 Global Wealth Report from Credit Suisse shows that the total global wealth has reached $317 trillions (circa $41,000/person), which is encouraging, and all this wealth must be used only for peace.

Like in any big family, there are differences, because some work more, some spend less, some move faster, and, especially, some are sick – this is the main reason for differences: not all people can be equally sick, some people are sicker than others. However, all the people and the government will work to help each other.

It is a major responsibility of the Government to increase the global wealth, and to train those in need, to have better working abilities and opportunities.

USA, UC Berkeley (1868, motto Fiat lux), from Campanile (1914, 94 m) looking north-northwest: Mathematics Dep. and Economics Dep. (right middle), Civil Engineering Dep. (next back), Nanofabrication Lab. (next back), Transportation Inst. (center left), Earth Sciences and Map Library and Seismological Lab (next left), Graduate School of Journalism (next back), Center for Developing Economies (next right), Memorial Glade (green center left).

Question 49. Was the bureaucracy dominating everything in 633 in Persia?

Response: Yes, and the usual war errors - for 11 years, 633 – 644, Rashidun Caliphate (first Muslim Caliphate) had wars against neighbors in Persia, Levant (Eastern Mediterranean region), and Egypt, and occupied them.

No bureaucracy – this is required by all people, and every day attention will be given for improvements in this direction.

In a well-organized country, with all people working together in harmony, this can be accomplished in several years.

Constant attention will be focused on avoiding duplication at all levels of the world government – there must be continuous collaboration between all levels, to prevent duplication, and to eliminate it, if it was found.
A vice is nourished by being concealed (from Latin: Alitur vitium vivitque tegendo).

Question 50. Was there corruption in 680, in the Eastern Roman Empire?

Response: Sure, plenty, plus the war errors - for 675 years, 680 – 1355, the Eastern Roman Empire had wars with the Bulgarian Empire (in Bulgaria and around).

Everybody will work really hard to completely eliminate corruption, organized crime, cybercrime and drug trafficking.

Italy, Roma, the river Tiber (Tevere, moving from back to front), the Mausoleum of Hadrian (left, 134-139, Hadrian (76-138), after 650 wrongly called Castel Sant'Angelo) and the Pons Aelius (134 AD, 135 m, 7 m height, 5 spans, with 10 sculptures).

Question 51. Any ideas about interest on their savings in 711 in Hispania?

Response: Not much, busy with war mistakes - for 7 years, 711 – 718, Umayyad Caliphate (Muslims from Persia to North Africa) had wars against Visigothic Kingdom (in Hispania), and occupied Hispania.

Each government department will have some reserves for special situations (natural disasters, big accidents), and the banks will also have good financial reserves.

All people will be encouraged to save some money in banks with 5% interest.

Italy, Rome (753 BC), the northwest side of Amphitheatrum Flavium (80, started by Flavius Vespasian (born 9 AD, emperor 69-79) in 70, and completed by his son Titus Flavius Vespasianus (born 39, emperor 79-81) in 80, wrongly called Colosseum).

Question 52. Is there concern regarding integrity and efficiency in 772 in the Frankish Empire?

Response: Not at all, just more war errors - for 32 years, 772 – 804, Frankish Empire had wars with Saxons.

Inspectors will help the Government with the integrity and efficiency issues – always there are ways to improve the work.

Inspectors will give advice regarding integrity and efficiency, and will take corrective actions when necessary.

Paris (250 BC): l'Hôtel de Ville (City Hall since 1357, King Francis I started this building in 1533, finished 1628, 1873-1892

Question 53. Will family assistance have priority in 793 western Europe?

Response: Unfortunately, no, because of the many war errors - for 147 years, 793 – 940, Vikings (from southern Scandinavia) attacked and invaded the British Isles, Ireland, Francia, Spain and Portugal.

Because all families need assistance from time to time, and the big 7.7 B family on Earth contains billions of small families, all of them will have the assistance they need – this will be the result of one country well organized and managed.

From the Shard (244 m), looking west to (from right down): railroad bridge (Cannon St Station), Southwalk Bridge, Millennium Bridge, another railroad bridge, Blackfriars Bridge, and Waterloo Bridge.

Question 54. Are there abuses in 862 in Europe?

Response: Plenty, and big war errors - for 111 years, 862 – 973, the second Hungarian (from the Ural Mountains) invasions of Europe (Bulgaria, Eastern Roman Empire, Serbia, Croatia, Francia, Italia, Spain)

It is a demanding effort, after thousands of years of all kinds of abuses, but the abuses will be gone!

Special attention will be given by Advisors to avoid abuses and wrong interpretations of the rules. All assistants (doctors, mathematicians, CEOs, engineers and teachers) will closely monitor all activities, to avoid abuses and wrong interpretations of the rules.

This requirement of not having abuses is demanding – but this is a general job, not only for Government, but for everybody, as part of the big family, we just don't need abuses.

The abuse, in some places, of confiscating the land by some government bureaucrats will be eliminated – the land belongs to the people, not the government.

The abuse, in some places, of having trains, airplanes, and others making unhealthy noises, with the government support, will be eliminated – peoples' health has always priority.

The abuse, in some places, of having to change the clocks twice a year will be eliminated – only the normal local time zones will be used.

If abuses are observed, they will be immediately reported to the Government, and corrected, in general, by the People Assistance Department, which will have personnel, including medical assistants, to analyze and promptly solve the abuses.

Question 55. What about commerce in 864 in the Russkiy Khaganate?

Response: Always there was some forms of commerce everywhere, because people wanted to collaborate with each other in peace, but the rulers were making war errors all the time - for 177 years, 864 – 1041, the Russkiy Khaganate (large area around Kiev) had raids on the Caspian Sea shores.

In one country, with one market, the commerce between the people on Earth will be free of taxes, tariffs, duties, etc. – plenty of opportunities for everybody.

USA, Boston (founded in 1630): tall ships from many countries, at the Boston Fish Pier (opened in 1915).

Question 56. Was the speech free and responsible in 1000 in southern Italy?

Response: Not yet, because of too many war errors - for 139 years, 1000 – 1139, there were wars between cities in southern Italy.

The speech will be free and responsible. It is expected not to call for war, violence, or similar destructive activities. People want peace, freedom, health, friendship, harmony and prosperity for all.

Italy, ruins of Pompeii (650 BC, in 79 covered by ash), from Via Marina, houses west of Forum Pompeiorum, with Mt Vesuvius, 1281 m, 9 km northwest, back.

Question 57. Was the press free and responsible in 1015 in Georgia?

Response: Well, no press yet, because of the numerous war mistakes - for 45 years, 1015 – 1060, the Eastern Roman Empire had wars with the Kingdom of Georgia.

The press will be free and responsible. It is expected not to call for war, violence, or similar destructive activities. People want peace, freedom, health, friendship, harmony and prosperity.

Finland, Helsinki: a commercial harbor in the south-west of the city, near Hietalahdenranta, with the boat Aranda.

Question 58. Were some people protesting violently in 1048 in Eastern Europe?

Response: Regrettably yes, many times, plus the terrible war errors - for 260 years, 1048 – 1308, the Turco-Persian Sunni Muslim empire had wars with the Eastern Roman Empire.

People can assemble peacefully only, with police for help. It is expected not to call for war, violence, or similar destructive activities. People want peace, freedom, health, friendship, harmony and prosperity for all.

USA, New York: W 42nd Street, near 8th Avenue, with the Chrysler Building (1930, 320 m, 77 floors, center-right far back).

Question 59. Did people have jobs in 1051 in Japan?

Response: Yes, there were a few jobs, especially working for rulers, but the vast majority did not have jobs, mainly because of the very frequent war errors - for 12 years, 1051 – 1063, there were wars between different parts of Japan.

There will always be plenty of jobs at world minimum wage (assisting other people, for example), and the standard situation will be this: more jobs than available people, so people will choose the jobs they like the most.

France, Paris: The monument "Flamme de la Liberté" (1987, 3.5 m in height, a full-sized, gold-leaf-covered replica of the new flame at the upper end of the torch carried in the hand of the Statue of Liberty, New York), in Place de l'Alma, near the Pont de l'Alma, Paris.

Question 60. Were there beggars in 1066 in Normandy?

Response: Yes, everywhere, mostly because of the many war errors - for 99 years, 1066 – 1165, Normandy had wars with England and Wales.

No unemployment, no homelessness, no begging, no tipping – just all working harmoniously, having good houses, and helping each other.

Japan, Tokyo, Shinjuku. Center-left: Tokyo Opera City Tower (234 m, 54 fl, 1996); right Shinjuku Mitsui Building (224 m, 55 fl, 1974),

France, Paris: Nymph statues on an Art Nouveau lamp, on the west side of the Pont Alexandre III (1896-1900, for Alexander III (1845-1894), Emperor (Tsar) of Russia, King of Poland and Grand Prince of Finland (1881-1894), had concluded the Franco-Russian Alliance in 1892. His son Nicholas II (1868-1918, the last Russian Emperor (Tsar)) laid the foundation stone in October 1896), the most ornate bridge, which consists of a six-meter high single span steel arch.

Question 61. Could people improve the rules in 1096 in Europe?

Response: No way, because of the colossal war errors - for 195 years, 1096 – 1291, the Crusades (from France, Italy, Holy Roman Empire, Papal States, Norway, Venice, Spain, Portugal, England, etc.) were wars against the Turks and their allies.

The Constitution of the World can be improved when over 66% of the voters agree.

Obviously, there will appear in the future many more advanced technologies, medicines, etc., which will certainly create conditions to have more harmony, more collaboration, etc.

Italy, Venezia, Libreria Sansoviniana (left), Il Campanile (center-left), Palazzo Ducale (right), and a Japanese couple wedding picture.

Italy, Rome (753 BC, one of the oldest continuously occupied cities in Europe, called Roma Aeterna (The Eternal City) and Caput Mundi (Capital of the World)), Forum Romanum, the south part of the southeast side of Arcus Septimii Severi (right, 203, Septimius Severus (145 – 211)), the southeast part of Templum Saturni (center right, 497 BC, 42 BC, 380), the northwest part of Basilica Juliae (center left, 54 BC by Julius Caesar (100 – 44 BC).

Question 62. What was the purpose of the people on Earth in 1206 in Asia and Europe?

Response: Well, the purpose of the people was to stay alive in the middle of terrible war mistakes - for 131 years, 1206 – 1337, Mongol Empire invaded China, Korea, Vietnam, Japan, Russia, Eastern Roman Empire, Poland, Hungary, Bulgaria, Serbia, Croatia, Crusader states, Turks, Muslims.

The purpose for all people on Earth is to be healthy, to live in peace, freedom and harmony, to be prosperous, and to prepare to expand to the Moon, asteroids, Mars, and other places in the Universe, which can support life.

France, Paris: The Panthéon (1758 - 1790, 83 m height, mausoleum in the Latin Quarter in Paris, modeled on the Pantheon (126 AD) in Rome), seen from Rue Soufflot, near Rue Saint-Jacques.

Question 63. What were the immediate objectives for people in 1282 in southwest Europe?

Response: The immediate objectives for people were to escape from the enormous war errors - for 20 years, 1282 – 1302, Crown of Aragon (Spain) and Kingdom of Trinacria (Sicily, Italy) had wars against Napoli (Italia), France and Majorca (Spain) – it was called the war of the Sicilian Vespers, and 553 years later Giuseppe Verdi wrote the five-act Italian opera I Vespri Siciliani (1855).

Important immediate objectives for everybody are:
- Reserve time for happiness.
- Use robots and automated processes, work less, and spend more time with your family.
- The weekend will be like a small vacation.
- Prevent burnout.
- Make civilized behavior and harmony everywhere is an important issue.
- Eliminate stress.
- Help friends and colleagues.
- Keep everybody relaxed, calm, friendly, patient, and happy.

.

Question 64. Any ideas how to harmonize the world in 1337 in western Europe?

Response: Impossible, too many war mistakes - for 116 years, 1337 – 1453, France, Castile (Spain), Scotland, Genoa (Italy), Majorca (Spain), Bohemia (Germany), Aragon (Spain) and Brittany (near France) had wars (called Hundred Years' war) with England, Burgundy (in France), Aquitaine (southwest of France), Portugal, Navarre (north of Spain), Flanders (part of The Netherlands), Hainaut (part of Belgium), and Holy Roman Empire (Germany and neighbors from south).

Using cordiality, having peaceful discussions, using a balanced approach to all issues, being amicable, coordinating the work in teams, being pleasant and melodic, etc.

Italy, Rome (753 BC), Forum Romanum, the northwest side of Arcus Septimii Severi (left, 203, Septimius Severus (145 – 211)), the northeast part of Templum Saturni (center left, 497 BC, 42 BC, 380), Tabularium (78 BC, started by Quintus Lutatius Catulus (149 – 87 BC)) and Campidoglio right.

Question 65. Any books about a World Constitution in 1351 in China?

Response: Not one, just war errors - for 17 years, 1351 – 1368, the Ming dynasty in China had wars with the Yuan dynasty, successor of the Mongol Empire.

For better understanding and easier implementation of this harmony and the World Constitution, the following books, by Michael M. Dediu, are recommended:
- Our Future is Sustainable Peace and Prosperity – Moving from conflicts to harmony and peace
– Our Future Depends on Good World Educations – Moving from frail education to solid education.
– Friendly, Helpful & Smart World Management - Moving from bureaucracy to responsive world management
– If You Want Peace, Prepare for Peace! – Moving from preparation for war to preparation for peace
– World with One Country & its Ten Friendly Regions - Moving from 195 disagreeing countries, to 1 country with 10 collaborating regions
– After 10,000 Years of Conflicts, People want 10,000 Years of Harmony - Moving from continuous wars to stable peace
- The Constitution of the World – Moving from many unsustainable constitutions, to just one Constitution of the World
- World Constitution Implementation – Moving from violent changes, to smooth transition to the Constitution of the World
- It is getting truer and truer – we urgently need the World Constitution: Moving from anarchic changes, to balanced transition to the Constitution of the World
- World Constitution with Lovely Comments - Moving from many suboptimal constitutions to the much better Constitution of the World

More books are listed in bibliography.

Italy, Venezia: A small church on the Isola di San Michele, between Venezia and Murano. Around 1100, hermits of the Camaldolese Order occupied this island, and founded the Monastery of St. Michael. This monastery became a great center of learning and printing. The famous cartographer, Fra Mauro, whose maps were so crucial to the European exploration of the world, was a monk of this community. In his youth, Mauro had traveled widely as a soldier. He was familiar with the Middle East. He entered monastic life at a late stage in life. In the monastery, he became a mapmaker. By 1450 he created a great *mappamundi* (world map) of the Old World with surprising accuracy, including extensive written comments reflecting the geographic knowledge of his time. The map is known today as the "Fra Mauro map". A commemorative medal of the period describes Fra Mauro as "chosmographus incomparabilis". The monks were expelled in 1814, under Napoleon. The grounds then became Venice's major cemetery.

Question 66. Any ideas about what territories should have a World Constitution in 1356 in Western Europe?

Response: Not at all, only war errors - for 19 years, 1356 – 1376, Aragon (Spain) and France had wars with Castile (Spain) and England, Genoa, Portugal, Navarre and Granada.

The Constitution of the World is valid not only on Earth, but also on the space around Earth, on the Moon, Mars, asteroids and any other places where the very good people on Earth will be moving in the future.

France, Paris: Rue Soufflot (left, looking north-west to Jardin du Luxembourg (1612, left back)), near Rue Saint-Jacques (right), with Université Paris 1 Panthéon-Sorbonne (right).

Question 67. Any ideas about how long will the World Constitution be working, in 1367 in Vietnam?

Response: No, because of the war errors - for 23 years, 1367 – 1390, Champa (part of Vietnam) had wars with the rest of Vietnam.

The Constitution of the World is intended for at least 10,000 years of harmonious living on the happy Earth and many other places.

UK, London: From the southwest side of the Tower of London (left 180 m), looking south to the fortifications at the southwest corner of the third external western wall, and the City Hall (center left, after Thames).

Question 68. Any ideas about when will this World Constitution be ready to come into force, in 1453, in Constantinople?

Response: Unfortunately not, because of the so many war errors - in 1453 there was the fall of Constantinople, capital of the Eastern Roman Empire, after over 2,000 years of the Roman Empire, built on the Roman Republic. If the leaders before 1453 would not have made all the severe errors of having wars and conflicts, by 1453 people would have been at the level of civilization which we have now, 568 years later, in 2021 – just imagine how much better off we would be now, without all these major errors of the past!

The Constitution of the World is ready to come into force, and to be put into practice, for the benefit of all people on Earth, on 6 March 2020, and it is ready to remain into force, and enjoyed by all people, at least until 6 March 12020.

Bibliography

Michael M. Dediu is also the author of these books (which can be found on Amazon.com, and www.derc.com):

1. Aphorisms and quotations – with examples and explanations
2. Axioms, aphorisms and quotations – with examples and explanations
3. 100 Great Personalities and their Quotations
4. Professor Petre P. Teodorescu – A Great Mathematician and Engineer
5. Professor Ioan Goia – A Dedicated Engineering Professor
6. Venice (Venezia) – a new perspective. A short presentation with photographs
7. La Serenissima (Venice) - a new photographic perspective. A short presentation with many photos
8. Grand Canal – Venice. A new photographic viewpoint. A short presentation with many photos
9. Piazza San Marco – Venice. A different photographic view. A short presentation with many photos
10. Roma (Rome) - La Città Eterna. A new photographic view. A short presentation with many photos
11. Why is Rome so Fascinating? A short presentation with many photos
12. Rome, Boston and Helsinki. A short photographic presentation
13. Rome and Tokyo – two captivating cities. A short photographic presentation
14. Beautiful Places on Earth – A new photographic presentation
15. From Niagara Falls to Mount Fuji via Rome - A novel photographic presentation
16. From the USA and Canada to Italy and Japan - A fresh photographic presentation
17. Paris – Why So Many Call This City Mon Amour - A lovely photographic presentation

18. The City of Light – Paris (La Ville-Lumière) - A kaleidoscopic photographic presentation
19. Paris (Lutetia Parisiorum) – the romance capital of the world - A kaleidoscopic photographic view
20. Paris and Tokyo – a joyful photographic presentation. With a preamble about the Universe

UK, London, on Thames (flowing left to right), looking northeast to the steel suspension London Millennium Footbridge (1996-2000, 325 m).

Italy, Rome (753 BC, one of the oldest continuously occupied cities in Europe, called Roma Aeterna (The Eternal City) and Caput Mundi (Capital of the World)), in Piazza Quirinale, the northeast side of Fountain of Castor (1818), with Obelisco del Quirinale (or Monte Cavallo, 1786, 29 m, from Mausoleum of Augustus (63 BC-14 AD)), and statues of the Dioscuri (Castor and Pollux, twin sons of Zeus and Leda) from the thermal baths of Constantine (272-337), Opus Phidiai on the left.

21. From USA to Japan via Canada – A cheerful photographic documentary
22. 200 Wonderful Places, In The Last 50 Years – A personal photographic documentary
23. Must see places in USA and Japan - A kaleidoscopic photographic documentary
24. Grandeurs of the World - A kaleidoscopic photographic documentary
25. Corneliu Leu – writer on the same wavelength as Mark Twain. An American viewpoint
26. From Berkeley to Pompeii via Rome – A kaleidoscopic photographic documentary
27. From America to Europe via Japan - A kaleidoscopic photographic documentary
28. Discover America and Japan - A photographic documentary
29. J. R. Lucas – philosopher on a creative parallel with Plato, An American viewpoint
30. From America to Switzerland via France - A photographic documentary
31. From Bretton Woods to New York via Cape Cod - A photographic documentary
32. Splendid Places on the Atlantic Coast of the U. S. A. - A photographic documentary
33. Fourteen nice Cities on three Continents - A photographic documentary
34. 17 Picturesque Cities on the World Map - A photographic documentary
35. Unforgettable Places from Four Continents, including Trump buildings - A photographic documentary
36. Dediu Newsletter, Volume 1, Number 1, 6 December 2016 – Monthly news, review, comments and suggestions for a better and wiser world
37. Dediu Newsletter, Volume 1, Number 2, 6 January 2017 (available also at www.derc.com).
38. Dediu Newsletter, Volume 1, Number 3, 6 February 2017 (available at www.derc.com).
39. London and Greenwich, - A photographic documentary
40. Dediu Newsletter, Volume 1, Number 4, 6 March 2017 (available also at www.derc.com).

Rome: Accademia Nazionale dei Lincei (1603, the oldest worldwide) has its library in Palazzo Corsini (1740), Via della Lungara 10, Roma.

41. Dediu Newsletter, Volume 1, Number 5, 6 April 2017 (available also at www.derc.com).
42. Dediu Newsletter, Volume 1, Number 6, 6 May 2017 (available also at www.derc.com).
43. Dediu Newsletter, Volume 1, Number 7, 6 June 2017 (available also at www.derc.com).
44. London, Oxford and Cambridge, A photographic documentary
45. Dediu Newsletter, Volume 1, Number 8, 6 July 2017 (available also at www.derc.com).
46. Dediu Newsletter, Volume 1, Number 9, 6 August 2017 (available also at www.derc.com).
47. Dediu Newsletter, Volume 1, Number 10, 6 September 2017 (available also at www.derc.com).
48. Three Great Professors: President Woodrow Wilson, Historian German Arciniegas, and Mathematician Gheorghe Vranceanu – A chronological and photographic documentary
49. Dediu Newsletter, Volume 1, Number 11, 6 October 2017 (available also at www.derc.com).
50. Dediu Newsletter, Volume 1, Number 12, 6 November 2017 (available also at www.derc.com).
51. Dediu Newsletter, Volume 2, Number 1 (13), 6 December 2017 (available also at www.derc.com).
52. Two Great Leaders: Augustus and George Washington - A chronological and photographic documentary
53. Dediu Newsletter, Volume 2, Number 2 (14), 6 January 2018 (available also at www.derc.com).
54. Newton, Benjamin Franklin, and Gauss, A chronological and photographic documentary
55. Dediu Newsletter, Volume 2, Number 3 (15), 6 February 2018 (available also at www.derc.com).
56. 2017: World Top Events, But Many Little Known, A chronological and photographic documentary
57. Dediu Newsletter, Volume 2, Number 4 (16), 6 March 2018 (available also at www.derc.com).
58. Vergilius, Horatius, Ovidius, and Shakespeare - A chronological and photographic documentary.
59. Dediu Newsletter, Volume 2, Number 5 (17), 6 April 2018 (available also at www.derc.com).

USA, Boston: a view of the north-east part of Boston, from Cambridge, over Charles River Basin. Federal Reserve Bank Building (187 m, left), and other tall buildings in the financial district.

60. Dediu Newsletter, Volume 2, Number 6 (18), 6 May 2018 (available also at www.derc.com).
61. Vivaldi, Bach, Mozart, and Verdi - A chronological and photographic documentary.
62. Dediu Newsletter, Volume 2, Number 7 (19), 6 June 2018 (available also at www.derc.com).
63. Dediu Newsletter, Volume 2, Number 8 (20), 6 July 2018 (available also at www.derc.com).
64. Dediu Newsletter, Volume 2, Number 9 (21), 6 August 2018 (available also at www.derc.com).
65. World History, a new perspective - A chronological and photographic documentary.
66. World Humor History with over 100 Jokes, a new perspective - A chronological and photographic documentary
67. Dediu Newsletter, Volume 2, Number 10 (22), 6 September 2018 (available also at www.derc.com).
68. Dediu Newsletter, Volume 2, Number 11 (23), 6 October 2018 (available also at www.derc.com).
69. Dediu Newsletter, Volume 2, Number 12 (24), 6 November 2018
70. Da Vinci, Michelangelo, Rembrandt, Rodin - A chronological and photographic documentary
71. Dediu Newsletter, Volume 3, Number 1 (25), 6 December 2018
72. Dediu Newsletter, Volume 3, Number 2 (26), 6 January 2019
73. From Euclid to Edison – revelries in the past 75 years - A chronological and photographic documentary
74. – Socrates to Churchill Aphorisms celebrated after 1960 - A chronological and photographic documentary
75. - Dediu Newsletter, Volume 3, Number 3 (27), 6 February 2019
76. – Hippocrates to Fleming: Medicine History celebrated after 1943 - A chronological and photographic documentary
77. - Dediu Newsletter, Volume 3, Number 4 (28), 6 March 2019
78. - Dediu Newsletter, Volume 3, Number 5 (29), 6 April 2019
79 – Archimedes to Ford: Invention History celebrated after 1943 - A chronological and photographic documentary
80 - Dediu Newsletter, Volume 3, Number 6 (30), 6 May 2019
81 – Sutherland to Pavarotti: Great Singers History - A chronological and photographic documentary
82 - Dediu Newsletter, Volume 3, Number 7 (31), 6 June 2019

A south-west view of Rome from Altare della Patria: Theatrum Marcelli (the Theatre of Marcellus (Marcus Claudius Marcellus, 42 BC – 23 BC, Emperor Augustus' nephew), 13 BC, left back).

83 - Dediu Newsletter, Volume 3, Number 8 (32), 6 July 2019
84 – Augustus to Rockefeller: History of the Wealthiest People - A chronological and photographic documentary
85 - Dediu Newsletter, Volume 3, Number 9 (33), 6 August 2019
86 – Pythagoras to Fermi: History of Science - A chronological and photographic documentary
87 - Dediu Newsletter, Volume 3, Number 10 (34), 6 September 2019
88 – Our Future is Sustainable Peace and Prosperity – Moving from conflicts to harmony and peace
89 - Dediu Newsletter, Volume 3, Number 11 (35), 6 October 2019 – World Monthly Report with news
90 – Our Future Depends on Good World Educations – Moving from frail education to solid education
91 - Dediu Newsletter, Volume 3, Number 12 (36), 6 November 2019 – World Monthly Report with News and Suggestions for Sustainable Peace, Freedom and Prosperity
92 – Friendly, Helpful & Smart World Management - Moving from bureaucracy to responsive world management
93 – If You Want Peace, Prepare for Peace! – Moving from preparation for war to preparation for peace
94 - Dediu Newsletter, Volume 4, Number 1 (37), 6 December 2019 – World Monthly Report with News and Suggestions for Sustainable Peace, Freedom and Prosperity
95 – World with One Country & its Ten Friendly Regions - Moving from 195 disagreeing countries, to 1 country with 10 collaborating regions
96 - Dediu Newsletter, Volume 4, Number 2 (38), 6 January 2020 – World Monthly Report with News and Suggestions for Sustainable Peace, Freedom and Prosperity
97 – After 10,000 Years of Conflicts, People want 10,000 Years of Harmony - Moving from continuous wars to stable peace
98 - Dediu Newsletter, Volume 4, Number 3 (39), 6 February 2020 – World Monthly Report with News and Suggestions for Sustainable Peace, Freedom and Prosperity
99 – The Constitution of the World – Moving from many unsustainable constitutions, to just one Constitution of the World

Paris (founded circa 250 BC): L'Hôtel National des Invalides (1678), in the 7th arrondissement, with military museums (including details about Lafayette) and monuments, and the burial site for Napoleon Bonaparte, 1769-1821, 52.

100 - Dediu Newsletter, Volume 4, Number 4 (40), 6 March 2020 – World Monthly Report with News and Suggestions for Sustainable Peace, Freedom and Prosperity
101 - Dediu Newsletter, Volume 4, Number 5 (41), 6 April 2020 – World Monthly Report
102 - Dediu Newsletter, Volume 4, Number 6 (42), 6 May 2020 – World Monthly Report
103 – World Constitution Implementation – Moving from violent changes, to smooth transition to the Constitution of the World
104 - Dediu Newsletter, Volume 4, Number 7 (43), 6 June 2020 – World Monthly Report
105 - Dediu Newsletter, Volume 4, Number 8 (44), 6 July 2020 – World Monthly Report
106 - It is getting truer and truer – we urgently need the World Constitution: Moving from anarchic changes, to balanced transition to the Constitution of the World
107 - Dediu Newsletter, Volume 4, Number 9 (45), 6 August 2020 – World Monthly Report
108 - World Constitution with Lovely Comments - Moving from many suboptimal constitutions to the much better Constitution of the World
109 - Dediu Newsletter, Volume 4, Number 10 (46), 6 September 2020 – World Monthly Report
110 – World Constitution with Questions & Answers – Moving from many obsolete constitutions to the much better Constitution of the World
111 - Dediu Newsletter, Volume 4, Number 11 (47), 6 October 2020 – World Monthly Report
112 - World Projects - Moving from minor projects to great projects for the World
113 - Dediu Newsletter, Volume 4, Number 12 (48), 6 November 2020 – World Monthly Report
114 - Dediu Newsletter, Volume 5, Number 1 (49), 6 December 2020 – World Monthly Report
115 - World Opportunities for All - Moving from few local jobs, to world opportunities for all
116 - Dediu Newsletter, Volume 5, Number 2 (50), 6 January 2021 – World Monthly Report

USA, New York: On Broadway at 43rd St, looking southwest, in Times Square

117 - Self-Managing World - Moving from local ruling top-down, to self-managing world
118 – We are all in the same space boat – Peaceful Terra; Moving from local fragile boats to the solid Peaceful Terra
119 - Dediu Newsletter, Volume 5, Number 3 (51), 6 February 2021 – World Monthly Report
120 - All people ask for Peace + Freedom = Prosperity, Moving from local conflicts to world peace and freedom
121 - Dediu Newsletter, Volume 5, Number 4 (52), 6 March 2021 – World Monthly Report
122 - To pour Peace from a cup full of arms, MELT ALL ARMS! - Moving from arms race, to peace enjoyment
123 - Dediu Newsletter Vol 5, Number 5 (53), 6 April 2021 – World Monthly Report
124 - Bureaucracy is growing like a weed - People want a Quality Change; Yup, that's right! Better life for all!
125 - Dediu Newsletter Vol 5, Number 6 (54), 6 May 2021
126 – What is Life for Homo Sapiens post 2020? – Life is evolution by harmony, not by natural selection for people.
127 - Dediu Newsletter Vol 5, Number 7 (55), 6 June 2021 – World Monthly Report

Italy, Venezia - The south of La Piazzetta, the south of Piazza San Marco, with gondole, and wedding pictures of a Japanese couple.

USA, New York (1624): on Broadway, close to Times Square, and to Times Square Tower (2004, 221 m, 47 floors).

www.ingramcontent.com/pod-product-compliance
Lightning Source LLC
LaVergne TN
LVHW052251100826
845147LV00001B/15

* 9 7 8 1 9 5 0 9 9 9 3 9 2 *